EVERYDAY LIFE IN
ANCIENT ROME

LIONEL CASSON

Everyday Life in Ancient Rome

Revised and Expanded Edition

THE JOHNS HOPKINS UNIVERSITY PRESS
Baltimore and London

Originally published in 1975 as *The Horizon Book of Daily Life in Ancient Rome.*

© 1975, 1998 by American Heritage, a division of Forbes Inc.

New material © 1998 The Johns Hopkins University Press

Printed in the United States of America on acid-free paper

9   8   7   6   5   4   3   2   1

The Johns Hopkins University Press
2715 North Charles Street
Baltimore, Maryland 21218-4363
www.press.jhu.edu

Library of Congress Cataloging-in-Publication Data

Casson, Lionel. 1914–
    Everyday life in ancient Rome / Lionel Casson.
    p.   cm.
    Rev. ed. of: The Horizon book of daily life in ancient Rome. [1975]
    Includes bibliographical references and index.
    ISBN 0-8018-5991-3 (alk. paper). — ISBN 0-8018-5992-1 (pbk. : alk. paper)
    1. Rome—Social life and customs.   2. Rome—History—Empire, 30 B.C.–284 A.D.   I. Casson, Lionel. 1914–   Horizon book of daily life in ancient Rome.   II. Title.
DG78.C37   1998
937—dc21   98-19972
                                                                                      CIP

A catalog record for this book is available from the British Library.

To Luca

CONTENTS

ILLUSTRATIONS

PREFACE

This book presents a series of concise sketches of key phases of life in the Roman world during its greatest period, the peaceful and prosperous years of the first and second centuries A.D.: what life was like in the city, in the countryside, on the road; what it was like in the various levels of society, from the slave to the aristocrat, from the soldier in the ranks to his commander in chief, the emperor; what gods people put their faith in, what amusements beguiled them. The sketches are fashioned to reveal how the inevitable cycle from birth to death that we all share played out in the circumstances of this very special age.

The book originally appeared in 1975 as *Daily Life in Ancient Rome*. For this republication, I have added two chapters, supplied complete documentation (in a section at the back keyed to the text by page references and brief clues), and made a number of minor corrections and adjustments.

When sums of Roman money are quoted they have alongside them an amount in dollars to give some idea of the equivalent purchasing power. These amounts are by no means to be taken as exact. Converting ancient values into modern is highly speculative; what I offer are little more than guesses based on the handful of useful indications of ancient wages and commodity prices that have survived. I am fairly certain, however, that they do not overestimate, though they may underestimate.

EVERYDAY LIFE IN
ANCIENT ROME

The Times

"In the second century of the Christian Era, the empire of Rome comprehended the fairest part of the earth, and the most civilized portion of mankind. The frontiers of that extensive monarchy were guaranteed by ancient renown and disciplined valor. The gentle, but powerful, influence of laws and manners had gradually cemented the union of the provinces. Their peaceful inhabitants enjoyed and abused the advantages of wealth and luxury. . . . During a happy period of more than fourscore years, the public administration was conducted by the virtue and abilities of Nerva, Trajan, Hadrian, and the two Antonines."

These are the words with which Edward Gibbon opens his monumental history. They paint a picture of material well-being whose colors, though perhaps too bright, are not false. It indeed was an age of peace and prosperity, thanks to the honesty and efficiency of Rome's government, the extent of its sway, and the strength of the armies with which it defended all it held.

The Mediterranean, most of what is today France, Spain, Belgium, Holland, the Balkan countries, even the better part of the British Isles, was one world politically, all under the rule of the Roman Empire. Any inhabitant could make his way from the burning sun of Mesopotamia to the mists of Scotland without crossing a national frontier. The founder of this vast realm, the man who welded it together, fashioned its machinery of government, and launched it on its incredibly long career, was Augustus, the grandnephew of Julius Caesar.

Augustus rode to power on the waves of bloody civil war, a series of large-scale bitter conflicts in which he first destroyed his great-uncle's assassins, Brutus and Cassius, and then his own partner in this success, Mark Antony. When, in 30 B.C., the latter fell on his sword and his celebrated supporter pressed an asp to her bosom, Augustus was left in sole command of the Roman world. From the arts of war he turned, with equal ability, to the arts of peace. And since fate kindly granted him almost half a century more of life, until A.D. 14, he was able to get the new arrangements he devised for governing Rome working smoothly and surely.

What he created was, basically, an autocracy—but one that functioned behind the façade of a republic. From roughly 500 B.C. to 50 B.C., when Julius Caesar in effect brought it to an end, Rome had been a republic. Its chief legislative body was a Senate (whose membership, though theoretically open to all, tended to be mostly drawn from the aristocracy), its chief executive a pair of annually elected consuls. Under Augustus the consuls and other magistrates of the republic continued to hold office, the Senate to sit regularly and deliberate and pass motions. But the reins of power, no doubt about it, were in Augustus's grasp. It was he who controlled the army and navy, who determined foreign and domestic policy, whose favor made or broke political careers, who appointed the administrators to run Rome's provinces, as the overseas possessions were called, who above all stood for the government in the eyes of both citizens and subjects. His face appeared on the coins they handled, his name was prominent on public buildings and monuments, and in all major communities there were temples where he or his *genius,* his "spirit," was worshiped. He was an emperor in all but name; he discreetly insisted on being called by the informal title *Princeps,* a neutral term that meant only "First Citizen."

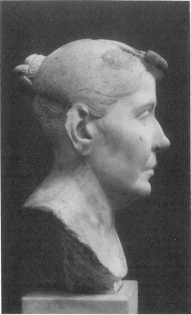

Romans. a) Pompey the Great, 106–48 B.C. b) Roman man, third century A.D. c) Roman woman, first century A.D. Ny Carlsberg Glyptothek, Copenhagen.

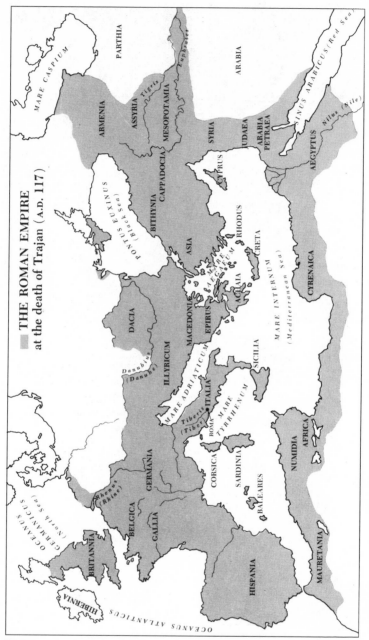

Map of the Roman Empire, ca. A.D. 117.

Augustus did his work so well that those who followed him on the throne—Tiberius, Claudius, Nero, Vespasian, and on through the great emperors of the second century A.D. whom Gibbon singled out for mention—merely adjusted or adapted but never basically changed what he had wrought. Obviously, there was no place in the system for freedom of speech or similar precious political rights that autocracy cannot countenance; on the other hand, as we shall see, infinitely more people enjoyed social and economic freedom than ever had under the republic. Moreover, Rome was, by and large, lucky in the quality of the rulers that came to the throne. Augustus's successors for the next two hundred years were all men of ability and, with a few exceptions, men of integrity. Even the few exceptions caused no fatal damage, since the governmental machinery continued to work in spite of them: a Caligula could spread terror in the capital with his insanities or a Nero helpless exasperation with his inanities, but the bureaucracy they headed went right ahead doing its job, collecting taxes, administering justice, carrying on the imperial correspondence, paying the imperial salaries—attending, in short, to the day-to-day needs of the state.

The key to the emperor's power—and to the peace enjoyed by the diverse peoples he ruled—was Rome's efficient armed forces. Before Augustus, Roman armies and navies had been called up as needed; Augustus created a standing army and navy, with himself, it goes without saying, as commander in chief. This was a potentially dangerous instrument, and the time would come when the imperial armies made, rather than obeyed, emperors. But that lay far in the future. The rulers of the first two centuries A.D. used the armed forces with care and intelligence, the army to conquer up to naturally defensible frontiers and then stand guard there, the navy to keep the sea lanes free of pirates.

The emperors lived in great palaces that they built for themselves on Rome's Palatine Hill. These included not only their living quarters but the grandiose halls where they held court and the welter of offices where their bureaucracy carried on the daily routine of government. Italy enjoyed a privileged status as Rome's historic heartland and the source of the superb soldiers that had enabled it to conquer the Mediterranean world, but Rome's strength now lay in its provinces; from these it drew the major portions of its wealth, brains, and muscle. The grain and wine and oil that fed its armies and civil servants came from Egypt and France and Spain; the businessmen who maintained its active commerce were largely provincials; and the army, though its core was still Italian, was increasingly recruited from the provinces, while provincials officered, as well as manned, the navy. By the second century A.D. the emperors themselves came from the provinces: Trajan and Hadrian were both of Spanish extraction. The head of state had to be as concerned for the political and economic health of Gauls, Arabs, Egyptians, and so on, as of Romans or Italians. When an ambitious provincial governor forwarded to Tiberius more in taxes than the stipulated amount, the emperor snapped that he wanted his "sheep sheared not skinned."

To administer the overseas territories so vital to the empire, Augustus and his successors sought men of ability whom they could trust. Willy-nilly they had to turn to the members of the Senate, even though few of these nourished very warm feelings toward the rulers who had, in a real sense, usurped the power they once held. The emperors, however, as soon as they were able, spread their net wider to entice into government service men of talent wherever they could find them. They drew upon well-established, well-to-do families that had previously stayed out of politics, upon provincials, even upon ex-slaves. In the process they made government service into a ready way for men of intelligence and ambition to climb up the social and political ladder.

But it was not only the man near the top who found paths for advancement open to him. They lay open for the whole of society, little people as well as big. This was because of Rome's unique attitude toward citizenship, its willingness to share it with others.

In ancient Athens only the children of Athenian parents were citizens. For a foreigner to gain the privilege took nothing less than an act of the Athenian Congress. Other ancient states were scarcely more charitable. Rome was an outstanding exception. From its very beginnings it adopted the practice of incorporating into the state some of the communities it conquered by granting them citizenship en bloc—more or less the way, *mutatis mutandis,* the United States has given its citizenship to Puerto Rico and Hawaii. What the republic had started, the emperors continued on an increased scale, turning by decree the populace of entire cities, even groups of cities, into Roman citizens overnight. Claudius was particularly generous in this regard; one wag grumbled that he had "put every Greek, Gaul, Spaniard, and Briton into togas." Citizenship, of course, brought with it the full protection of Rome's authority and law. The best-known instance is Saint Paul's refusal to be judged by a provincial governor; though a native of Tarsus in southern Asia Minor, he was a Roman citizen and demanded, as was his right, to be tried in Rome (how he became a citizen is a question; Tarsus may have been enfranchised en masse, perhaps by Julius Caesar in return for the help its people gave him during his fight to the death with Pompey). And, just as important, citizenship brought a man new social and economic opportunities, the possibility of entering and moving up in Rome's governmental apparatus. So we find people of provincial extraction, Greeks or Arabs or Levantines or any other of the many nationalities within Rome's bounds, mounting the ladder to administer its provinces, command its armies, even sit on its throne.

Enfranchisement of communities was only one of the large-scale ways in which Rome extended its citizenship. Another was through the manumission of slaves. Roman law had the incredibly liberal provision that the slave of a Roman citizen, upon being freed, became a citizen himself. Since the Romans commonly did free their slaves, multitudes of new members of the most varied origins each year joined the citizen body. Moreover, for whoever had the ambition there were any number of ways of becoming a citizen: by joining the army or the navy or by serving as a local magistrate in one's home town. By the beginning of the third century A.D. practically all the population of the empire had in one way or another gained citizenship. The ruling class was no longer Roman, not even Italian, but a mélange of men from all the provinces. Rome's empire lasted far longer than any other in history, half a millennium in the West and a millennium and a half in the East. Unquestionably one of the factors that held it together so successfully for so many years was the generous spread of the citizenship: men who were born in the mountains of Spain or on the shores of Syria came to feel themselves as Roman as those born along the Tiber; they were able to proclaim, as proudly as Paul, "*Civis romanus sum.*"

There were also strong economic ties to add their holding power. Augustus recognized that efficient rule over a large area required swift and easy movement of dispatches and troops. And so he and his successors embarked on a program that laced the empire together with a superb network of roads. At the same time, the navy finally freed the Mediterranean from its age-old curse of piracy and permitted ships to shuttle securely along its sea lanes. All this quickened economic life enormously. Towns now had easier access by road to local markets, and new access by road and ship to markets all over the empire. Soldiers wore armor of Austrian iron or of Spanish copper alloyed with British tin, wealthy men had themselves buried in coffins of Greek or Asia Minor marble, Italians drank wine from France and ate bread made of Egyptian grain, altars all over smoked with incense from Arabia or Ethiopia. More people than ever before were in a position to make money, as importers, exporters, shipowners, brokers, teamsters, and the myriad other activities needed by a vigorous and multifarious trade. Every center of consequence now boasted a comfortable middle class, and wealth in general came to be spread far wider than in previous ages. There was still an abyss between the very rich and the very poor, there were still throngs mired in desperate poverty, but previously only very few had been able to find an escape and now thousands did—and remained forever grateful to the government that had given them their chance.

The city of Rome was the nerve center of this great and prosperous realm. Under the emperors its population was perhaps as much as a million—a gigantic metropolis by any standards except those of today. After centuries of receiving immigrants and manumitted slaves into its midst, it had, like New York or San Francisco, become almost totally polyglot; by the second century A.D. perhaps 90 per cent of its denizens were of foreign extraction. Into its port came the products of Europe, Africa, Asia; in its public places stood buildings that only the rulers of an immensely wealthy state could afford to erect; its streets were thronged with men of all classes, with lofty officials and government slaves, with millionaire shipowners and bankers and a mass of chronic unemployed who lived off government handouts. It was the capital of a state that for the first and last time in history had made one unified political whole of the Mediterranean, that boasted a society more open than any before the nineteenth century and a prosperity unmatched until the twentieth, that gave Western civilization the longest period of peace it was ever to know.

Let us look at the various facets of life in this great capital during its finest hour, the second century A.D., the years that Gibbon lauded as a veritable golden age. We will have several helpful guides to show us about: Pliny the Younger, an eminently proper nobleman who left behind a collection of letters to his circle of eminently proper friends; Petronius, a most improper nobleman who wrote the *Satyricon,* the justly celebrated novel about the doings of a trio of scoundrels among the *nouveaux riches;* and Martial and Juvenal, masters of poetic satire who looked, the one with amused scorn and the other with sardonic rage, on the urban scene about them.

CHAPTER II

The Family

Throughout the whole of Rome's history, one feature remained constant—the family. The city grew to be an empire, the republic became an autocracy, old-fashioned religion yielded to frenetic new cults from the East, but, through it all, Roman society was based on the family, economic life was built around it, and its many complex problems continued to provide endless matter for debate among Roman lawyers.

At the head of every Roman family was the *paterfamilias,* "father of the family," the oldest male member. He was undisputed lord and master, with even the power of life and death over his sons and daughters—a right that, primitive though it may seem, took a long time to become a dead letter; there were cases on record of its being exercised as late as the first century B.C., though happily not after that. Another equally extraordinary right that he had he never lost: until the day he died he was sole owner of the family property. Sons, daughters, grandsons, granddaughters, none could legally have possessions of their own so long as they were in the power of a *paterfamilias;* it was all his—even the salary of, say, a grown-up son with a lucrative government post, or a legacy that might have come to a middle-aged daughter from a friend.

One would expect to hear of the younger generation exploding in exasperation at such an impossible state of affairs, but apparently it did not. Almost certainly some accommodation must have been worked out, though we have no idea of what it was. One factor no doubt helped—that life expectancy was short, that only the exception lived to a ripe old age; thus, in the normal course of events, most children did not remain too long in this anomalous position of being adult in years yet minor by law.

In one sense a *paterfamilias* never did lose his power of life and death: when a child was born, he alone—not necessarily in consultation with the mother—determined whether it was to live or be exposed to die. (Infanticide was practiced throughout ancient times among poor and rich, the poor to limit the number of mouths they had to feed, the rich the number of heirs who would divide up a handsome property; we shall have more to say on the subject later on.) And when the children were grown up, inevitably the *paterfamilias* arranged marriages for them. Legally he could insist only that they take a mate and not specify whom, but since the girls were married off when barely into their teens and the boys had no money they could call their own, it is hardly likely that either had much choice.

Girls married when they were twelve to fifteen, boys when slightly older. Marriages were arranged to carry on a family's name and preserve its property. Passion and romance played no part; men who needed extramarital relations went to whores, or if they had the money, elegant courtesans. We hear many lurid tales about adultery, orgies, and depraved carryings on, but this all took place among the upper crust, the Roman nightclub crowd. Marriage among responsible Romans was a serious matter, knit by a firm emotional bond. There was, of course, a legal bond, but no religious one. No church blessed a Roman union. Consequently to cohabit with a woman without being formally married was not "living in sin," but a recognized procedure. Even emperors did it. Marcus Aurelius, for example, the philosopher-emperor who ruled Rome from A.D. 161 to 180, when his wife died took the daughter of his wife's business agent as concubine rather than wife "so as not to introduce a stepmother over all the children." It was not unusual for an upper-class woman to set up a household with a mate of humble status, even a slave; it might start tongues wagging, but there was nothing irregular about it.

In arranging a marriage, the first topic the *paterfamilias* turned to was the dowry. Every bride had to supply one—but it always remained hers; if her husband died, or if the couple divorced, the dowry was returned, less a fraction for the upkeep of the children, possibly another fraction as penalty if she had misbehaved. Since women married so early, their chance of being widowed was great; without a dowry there could have been no possibility whatsoever of finding a new husband.

Once the dowry and lesser matters had been settled, the families arranged a betrothal, a ceremony in which the prospective bridegroom not only made his pledge but sealed it with gifts, most often a ring that was worn on the very same finger we use today (ancient savants claimed that there was a special nerve running from the ring finger to the heart). Theoretically a formal wedding was not necessary, merely a matter of tradition, but a Roman bride wanted it as much as her modern counterpart wants a church wedding. In picking the day one had to be very careful to avoid any of the considerable number that were of evil omen. All of May was out, and so was the first half of June—although the second half was favored. When the day came around the bride was given a special hairdo, was dressed in a special gown—a full-length white wool tunic that had been woven on an old-fashioned loom—and donned a special orange or yellow veil. The house was decorated with flowers and boughs of evergreen. A sacrifice might be carried out—it was not obligatory—the marriage contract was signed before ten witnesses, the couple joined hands to mark the cementing of the union—and everybody sat down to the wedding feast. The Roman satirist Juvenal sums it up with his usual brevity: "The contract's signed, all shout 'Best wishes,' and take their seats for a huge repast." Toward evening a procession conducted the bride to her new home: four boys whose parents were still alive accompanied her, one lighting the way with a torch of a special thorn bush, two by her side, the fourth carrying her spinning apparatus; all walked, caroling wedding songs, to the doorway, where the bride put fillets of wool on the doorposts and anointed them with oil; she was then lifted over the threshold and saluted her husband with the touching age-old phrase *Ubi tu Gaius, ego Gaia,* "Where you (are) John, there I, Mary."

However, Gaius and Gaia did not have to be with each other very long if they did not care to. Divorce among the Romans was simple and quick: either party merely uttered to the other the laconic Latin phrase *Tuas res tibi habeto,* "Keep what's yours for yourself," and the union was severed. Whatever children there were, being in the power of the *paterfamilias,* remained with the father. The dowry was returned—though this might take some time if, as frequently happened, the husband was short of cash. Cicero's letters show us both sides: while frantically trying to pay off Terentia, his wife of thirty years whom he had divorced to marry a young woman with a fortune, he was equally frantically trying to collect his daughter Tullia's dowry from her spendthrift ex-husband.

From the moment a bride crossed the threshold of her husband's home she was a *matrona,* a married woman, who would from then on dress with proper restraint and take care of running the household. What this involved depended on the family's social status. If it was low, she would move into a slum apartment—in Rome all but the very rich lived in apartment houses—where her daily routine must have been much like that of the wife in a tenement-dwelling family of today. If she was middle-class, she still moved into an apartment, although one with the space to accommodate a maid, a cook, and perhaps other household slaves. If she was of the aristocracy, she moved into a mansion that most likely housed not only her husband but many of his family— grandparents, uncles, aunts, and numbers of the family freedmen, that is, the slaves who had been granted their liberty yet, as was often the case, continued to live with their erstwhile master. In such an establishment there would be a veritable army of household slaves.

And whatever class she belonged to, she had the responsibility of the children—if there were any. One of the distinctive features of family life in this age was the practice of some sort of birth control, at least among the upper classes.

In the first and second centuries A.D. there was an abnormal rate of childlessness among Roman families, particularly the well-to-do. Augustus, his eye on every phase of his subjects' existence, even tried to rectify the situation by law. He used both the carrot and the stick: special privileges for women with three or more children (for example, they had the right to act legally for themselves instead of having to go through a male guardian), special penalties for bachelors and childless couples (for example, they could not be named as heirs in a will). One cause certainly was the predilection on the part of many upper-class males for homosexual relations. A more serious cause was a deliberate effort on the part of the women to avoid childbearing. How they did it is a question. Both abortion and contraception were known, but there is no way of telling to what extent they were practiced. Abortion was at the very least painful and could be dangerous. Contraception was preferable; but, though the medical writings of the period mention perfectly good devices (for example, inserting olive oil or honey or other clogging fluids in the vagina or using pessaries of wool), they often prescribe them along with others that are so totally absurd—one doctor, for example, endorses as "very effective" the wearing of "the liver of a cat in a tube on the left foot"—that it is doubtful how much useful knowledge circulated among ordinary married Roman couples. The courtesans the poets are always mooning about, who played the role in Roman life that geisha have in Japanese, must have had their techniques, and what they knew may have filtered back, by way of philandering husbands, to Roman society women, particularly the likes of Messalina and other notorious adulteresses of the age who were interested in carrying on affairs as well as avoiding children. Possibly women insisted on their husbands' and lovers' practicing *coitus interruptus,* one of the simplest forms of contraception, but there is no mention of it in any of the contemporary medical writings or any other writings, so we have no way of being sure.

Whatever the techniques, one by-product was a welter of wealthy people with no children to inherit their riches. This inevitably brought into being a swarm of fortune hunters, who fawned on childless couples, dogged the steps of bachelors and widowers, chased after widows and spinsters—and kept the pens of the Roman satirists busy. Here is a sample from Martial:

> "Gemellus is doing all he can
>   to make Maronilla his bride.
> He showers gifts, he sighs, he groans,
>   he begs her to decide."
> "I suppose she's very beautiful."
>   "God, no! Her looks could kill."
> "Then what's produced this passionate love?"
>   "A codicil in her will."

Horace, Juvenal, Petronius, and others have their say on the disagreeable subject, so, even allowing for the satirist's exaggeration, it clearly was a well-established feature of Roman life.

We mentioned above the practice of getting rid of unwanted infants by exposing them to die. Whatever abortion or contraception was practiced was almost certainly limited to the rich; on the other hand, all classes, but particularly the poor, resorted to exposure. It did not necessarily mean the child's death. Some of the most famous tales of ancient literature, such as the story of Oedipus or of Romulus and Remus, concern infants who were exposed and then rescued in the nick of time, and there are even a few important historical figures who started life this way. As a matter of fact, people found it profitable to be on the lookout for foundlings in order to raise them as slaves either for their own household or for sale. In Roman Egypt, and very likely elsewhere as well, they scavenged for them in the town dump, where it was the practice to abandon infants; in legal documents slaves are frequently designated as being "from the dump." Sometimes they did not have to rely on the haphazardness of the dump: there were poverty-stricken families willing, despite laws against it, to sell unwanted children into slavery. Both the government and private individuals tried to alleviate the situation by instituting child-assistance programs. The emperor Nerva, followed by Trajan, established funds in various localities, the proceeds of which were to pay for the upkeep of a given number of boys and girls—many more boys, as it happened, than girls, since the emperors had in mind the needs of the armed forces. Private philanthropists who set up foundations happily avoided any such discrimination. Here, for example, is a provision in the will of a certain wealthy woman of Terracina, a town on the coast of Italy about midway between Rome and Naples; it is a bequest

of one million sesterces [some $4 million] to the town of Terracina in memory of her son Macer, so that, out of the income from this money, child-assistance subsidies might be paid to one hundred boys and one hundred girls—to each citizen boy 5 *denarii* [some $80] each month, to each citizen girl 3 *denarii* each month, the boys up to sixteen years, the girls up to fourteen years.

Such forms of aid were not enough to correct the situation. We find Constantine in the fourth century bowing to the inevitable and allowing parents to sell children, presumably to slave nurseries.

The infant who escaped being exposed was given a name in a special ceremony on the eighth or ninth day after birth; then, sometime within the next thirty days, the father entered the name in the public register. In lower-class homes the mothers suckled the children, but in families that could afford it, they were turned over successively to slave wet nurses, nurses, and nannies. Childhood was much shorter then than now: for a Roman girl it ended, as we have noted, with marriage in the early teens; for a boy, about fourteen or a little later, when, in a formal public ceremony, he put aside the medallion he had worn about his neck as a mark of childhood and his child's toga with its scarlet hem. Until then, children did as they always have: the girls played with dolls, the boys with tops and hoops. They built things with building bricks (rather than wooden blocks); they enjoyed time-honored games that involved dice or nuts (instead of marbles); they played draughts; they tossed balls back and forth; they had pets—dogs and a variety of birds.

When they were six or seven they started to go to school. There was no publicly supported elementary education. A *magister* or *grammaticus,* a "schoolmaster," would set up a school, taking a fee from each of his pupils and teaching them in return the three R's in both Greek and Latin. Writing they practiced on waxed tablets, arithmetic problems they worked out with *abacus* and *calculi,* "counting board" and "counting pebbles." Sometimes there was not even a schoolroom. The little group would gather under one of the colonnades that surrounded the forum, where passersby could hear the shrill voices rehearsing their lesson—and, no doubt, the owners of the voices, the hurly-burly of the passersby. But the children must have resisted such distractions with all their might, since what Horace, Martial, Saint Augustine, and others remembered best in recalling their school days was the teacher's irascibility and quick hand with the rod. Nurses accompanied the girls to school, and special slaves, called *paedagogi* or "child-leaders," the boys. Secondary education—presumably for boys, since the girls were by this time at home learning the running of a household—lasted until thirteen or fourteen and took up grammar, syntax, and literature in both Latin and Greek. The curriculum concentrated, in Greek, on Homer, Aeschylus, Sophocles, Euripides, and Menander, the celebrated writer of comedies; in Latin, on Vergil, Horace, and Terence, the Latin follower of Menander.

The slaves of a family that was merely moderately well off, including those needed for the household chores and those for the children, might number as many as half a dozen, while the slaves in a great aristocrat's mansion could be counted in the hundreds. In previous centuries Rome's wars of conquest had brought back thousands of prisoners to supply the slave markets. During the long period of peace that the empire maintained, that source had disappeared, and most slaves were bred at home. Masters encouraged their slaves to mate, for the children could either be raised for the household staff or sold off to other families. Home-grown slaves had the great advantage over foreign imports of being native speakers of Latin, a language that Greeks and others found very hard to learn. Household slaves were by no means all menials; those who tutored the children, for example, were often far more cultured than their owners. (This was even more true of the slaves employed in government and business; when we deal with them, in Chapter 4, we will take up the general question of ancient slavery and how vastly different it was from the forms with which most of us are familiar.) A slave was allowed to put by money he had earned through tips, bonuses, or other means, and with this accumulation, his *peculium* as it was called, he could eventually buy his liberty. As a freedman, he had certain obligations to his former owner and, as mentioned above, very often continued living in the same house. In the spacious mansions of the great, the multitudinous slaves and freedmen no doubt had their own quarters. In the average middle-class family, inhabiting an apartment with more or less limited room, slaves slept either off the premises or on pallets laid down nightly on the kitchen or corridor floors.

The chores carried on by the household slaves were rather different from today's. Making the beds went quickly, since there were no sheets but just a pair of spreads that were not too frequently changed; there were no hose to wash, since this item of clothing was practically unknown in ancient times; there were no shoes to shine, since the standard footgear was the sandal; and, as we shall see later, dusting and sweeping were simple. On the other hand, they had to carry in water from wells, fountains, and cisterns and carry out refuse—including commodes full of human wastes, since lavatories were limited to the ground floor and even there were few and far between. Rome's apartment houses were three to four stories high, some still more; Roman slaves must have done as much hauling up and down stairs as the housemaids in Victorian London.

Marketing was done by the slaves, sometimes accompanied by the master—not the lady—of the house. Most of it was for dinner, since the other two meals were light. Breakfast, taken at dawn when people rose, was a mere bite, like the European's today, a bit of bread or cheese or both. Lunch, taken at noon, was also usually cold: bread, cheese or meat, some fruit, a glassful of wine. The dinner hour was about three in the afternoon—uncomfortably close to lunch by our standards, but apparently the Roman, with only two scant meals to sustain him since dawn, was ready to fill his belly. Besides, unless he belonged to the fast set, whose members might carouse until the cock crowed, he was in bed shortly after dark; burning the midnight oil to read or talk by was an expensive procedure to be indulged in only by the ambitious or the rich. Dinner varied according to family and occasion. The very poor, cramped in a single room that served as living room, dining room, and bedroom, prepared it over a charcoal brazier and ate it seated at a table nearby. Or they might buy dinner ready cooked, a cheap stew or a pot of vegetables, from one of the snack bars that lined the streets; these also supplied hot water for washing. The well-to-do almost always had a room set aside for dining, the *triclinium,* so called because it had three couches, each accommodating three people, arranged in U-shaped fashion around a table. On these the diners reclined, leaning on the left elbow and facing the table. To eat at one's ease this way was *de rigueur.* The mark of a cheap snack joint, for example, was that the customers sat; it was the equivalent of our eating perched on a bar stool. Dinner consisted, as today, of three courses: hors d'oeuvres, which might include olives, lettuce, leeks, mint, and other vegetables and herbs; main course, usually a variety of dishes—meats, fowl, fish—from which the diners selected; dessert of fresh fruit. Wine was served throughout, generously mixed with water, sometimes half and half, often two parts of wine to three of water; only alcoholics took it neat. This was the normal meal in an upper-class household, the kind served to the family with perhaps a few intimate friends. A dinner party was another matter.

As one ancient pundit put it, the Graces make a nice small dinner party, the Muses a nice large one—since nine diners nicely filled the places on the three couches in a *triclinium.* The number of courses could mount from the usual three to half a dozen or more; as a result, even a modest affair might last three hours, and an elaborate banquet double that. Each course offered a range of exotic and expensive selections.

The first might begin with sliced eggs, snails, sea urchins, oysters (the last item was a particular favorite). The main course often included pheasant or goose or peacock among the choices in fowl, boar or newborn kid in meat, lobster or mullet or lamprey or turbot in seafood. And no *vin ordinaire* would be served but the excellent Falernian from the hills between Rome and Naples or a prized imported wine, usually Greek. At a big banquet that Caesar once gave, there were two Italian wines, Falernian and Mamertine (from Sicily, near the Strait of Messina), and two Greek, Chian and Lesbian; it was a historic social occasion, the first time guests had been served as many as four different wines. Another touch that extravagant hosts went in for was chilling the wine with snow brought down from nearby mountains.

The total cost of an elaborate banquet, complete with rare delicacies and wines, could run to astronomical figures; Lucullus, the celebrated gourmet, once spent 200,000 sesterces (some $800,000) to feed Pompey and Caesar. On the other hand, a Roman host had a way of cutting corners denied to the modern: he was allowed to serve different food to different guests. Only the high and mighty enjoyed the turbot and the glasses of vintage Falernian; guests who did not count got treated quite differently. Juvenal the satirist apparently suffered this ignominy, to judge from the blast he lets loose on the subject. While the host's end of the table drank two of Italy's best vintages, Alban and Setian, those below the salt, as it were, got a wine that "even filthy rags would refuse to sop up," to say nothing of a human gullet. The first course for the host's favorites was "shrimp walled round with asparagus," for the pariahs "a crab [Romans disliked crab] hemmed in with half an egg." The favorites savored mullet caught in the distant waters off Corsica or Sicily, lamprey from the Strait of Messina, *foie gras,* and a huge boar garnished with truffles and the finest mushrooms; the pariahs were served "an eel, first cousin to a water snake, or something fished out of the Tiber, fat and juicy from living by the sewer outlet . . . and a dishful of toadstools." The meal closed with one end of the table eating apples that might have come from the Garden of the Hesperides, and the other the sort of rotten apples people fed to performing monkeys.

A proper dinner party always included entertainment. At a staid, respectable affair, the guests as they ate were treated to recitations of poetry—often the host's own—done by a specially trained slave, and music, either singers accompanied by the flute or lyre, or the solo instruments. Sometimes a professional storyteller spun amusing and edifying yarns. After dinner they relaxed over wine and beguiled the time with more or less serious conversation, playing riddles, laughing at the sallies of a professional jester, or gambling at dice or draughts. At less decorous affairs, the diners were entertained not only by singers but by dancers, actors, acrobats, and so on. And over the wine, the level could drop still lower: chorus girls and men doing seductive dances, lewd comics, even gladiatorial contests. The drinking tended to get out of hand; guests would pass out or throw up, and their poor slaves would have their hands full to clean them off and get them safely home.

There were a number of fixed occasions during the year when families traditionally held parties. Birthdays, no less than with us, called for a party and presents. The biggest event of the year was the Saturnalia, the pagan holiday that underlies Christmas. By the second century A.D. it had grown from one to seven days in length, lasting from December 17 to 23. Schools were closed, gifts were exchanged, and it was the season to be jolly. Everyone, children included, was allowed to play gambling games, no slaves could be punished, and the height of the fun came when these exchanged places with the masters and were themselves waited on, reclining in style in the *triclinium*.

Finally we come to death in the family. Then as now, there were undertakers to take over the unpleasant details, to tidy up the corpse, removing whatever might cause unpleasant impressions, and to dress it in the formal garment, the toga ("Let's admit it: in a large part of Italy no one wears a toga except when he's dead," complains Juvenal, lamenting the decline in good manners). An emperor received a full-scale funeral, like a modern head of state, with a solemn cortege that included a band of horn players, professional female mourners, actors who declaimed appropriate passages from tragedies or impersonated the deceased, and a line of men wearing the death masks and robes of office of his distinguished ancestors. The ordinary family simply had the undertaker furnish bearers to carry the body in a covered bier or coffin to the burial ground, followed by a procession of relatives, friends, and slaves freed in the will.

Interring the dead within city limits was forbidden by religious taboo. So the practice was adopted of burying them along the roads leading from the city gates—which is why we today see the remains of a line of ancient tombs on each side of the Via Appia after it leaves Rome. The ancients knew both cremation and inhumation, preferring now one and now the other. In the heyday of the Roman Empire, both were in vogue. Well-to-do families went in for mausoleums in which the various members were laid to rest, often in sarcophagi, elaborately carved stone coffins. Inscribed plaques identified who built the mausoleum and for whom and usually gave certain other details such as the exact size of the plot—presumably to ensure that no latecomers would encroach on it. (One pessimistic soul added to his plaque, "From this tomb let all fraud and lawyers be absent.") Some preferred graves marked by more or less elaborate tombstones. Paupers were laid to rest in whatever they could afford, for example, a grave made of flat building tiles and as marker the upper half of a discarded shipping jar.

Hundreds and thousands of tombstones and plaques have survived. Many were excavated by archaeologists, many extracted from later walls and structures where they had been used as building stone. They form one of the most fruitful sources of information we have about the Roman world. Ancient writers concentrate on the doings of the rich and powerful, and practically no official documents, tax registers or census rolls or the like, have survived to redress the balance. It is from epitaphs that we get clues as to how lesser folk fared, how they earned their living, what their familial relationships were. These confirm that the wild tales about the orgies and sexual high jinks of the upper crust reflect, for all the prominence given to them, only a minor part of Roman social history, that there were multitudes of people leading quiet family lives in this extended age of peace, multitudes like the prosperous tradesman who inscribed on his family vault:

To the spirits of the departed. You wanted to precede me, most sainted wife, and you have left me behind in tears. If there is anything good in the regions below (for I lead a worthless life without you), be happy there as well, sweetest Thalassia . . . my wife for forty years. Papirius Vitalis, of the painters' trade, her husband, built this for his incomparable wife, himself, and their family.

CHAPTER III

On the Farm

"As usual, I am asking your advice on a matter of business. There are now for sale some landed properties that border on mine and, as a matter of fact, run into them. They have many points that tempt me. . . . First, the gain in beauty by rounding off my holdings; then, the pleasure—to say nothing of the economy—of making one trip and expense serve for a visit to both properties and of keeping both under the same agent and practically the same managers. . . . It is 3,000,000 sesterces [some $12 million]. . . . True, I've practically all my funds tied up in land, but I have some cash on loan [money that could be called in], and borrowing presents no problem." So wrote Pliny the Younger to a friend about the turn of the first century A.D.

Where else were wealthy Romans to invest their capital if not in land? There were no such things as stocks and bonds. There was, to be sure, commerce, but that was risky, involving for the most part speculating in cargoes to be bought or sold abroad. Besides, commerce was for the moneygrubbers, whereas landed property was a gentleman's form of investment; it was where the best families had always put their money. And so, up and down Italy and throughout the provinces, farm acreage steadily passed into the hands of well-to-do absentee landlords; noblemen whose families had owned land for centuries accumulated yet more of it, and in their wake the *nouveaux riches,* like Petronius's rags-to-riches hero Trimalchio, began to acquire their maiden properties.

Over and above its social éclat, landowning was a sound form of investment. Though commerce and industry were thriving aspects of ancient economic life, both were minor compared with agriculture. Rome, Alexandria, Marseilles, Antioch, and Carthage were mighty ports whose docks and warehouses hummed with activity, but just a few miles inland from them, men lived almost totally off the land. Villages, towns, even great cities such as Milan or Lyons, were first and foremost agricultural centers serving, and kept alive by, the farms round about.

Multimillionaires preferred to invest in the provinces, where they could amass properties of well-nigh feudal dimensions. At one time in the first century A.D., fully half of what is today Tunisia belonged to a mere six owners. In France archaeologists have uncovered an estate that embraced twenty-five hundred acres; the farm buildings alone covered forty-five. But men of such wealth naturally were comparatively few. There were many more on Pliny's level, and these continued to put their money into Italy.

If they had in mind to invest in livestock—which almost always meant sheep and goats, to provide wool and hides for market—they would buy a large tract in the southern part of the peninsula, below Naples, where the poorish soil was more profitable to graze than to till. If their preference was crops, the alternatives were, by and large, grain, vines, or olives. Grain was, far more than now, the staff of life: from it came not only bread but the poor man's daily porridge. Wine, too, played a far greater role then: the ancients drank it before, after, and between meals, as well as during; it was their coffee and tea and spirits. And olive oil was their butter, soap, and electricity: they cooked with it, anointed themselves with it at the baths, and burned it in their lamps. For grain, the choicest lands were in the flat plains of the Po Valley or the Campania around Naples; for wine, the hilly country of the Piedmont or Tuscany or the hills about Rome was best; while the finest olives were grown near the northern border of Campania. Landowners tended to favor vines. Italy's wines commanded a good market up and down the peninsula and abroad as well, despite the high cost of transport (oxcart or donkeyback to the nearest port), whereas its grain and olives generally went no farther than the local markets.

There was one crucial decision to make: what kind of farm operation was it to be? A collection of family-sized plots for rental to tenants? Or big farms run by slave labor?

In certain cases there was no choice: large-scale grazing, for example, had to be done with slave shepherds and goatherds. Where the choice existed, there were pros and cons on each side. Renting to tenants had the advantage of reducing an owner's investment, since he did not have to put out the formidable sum it took to buy a staff of slaves. On the other hand, he rarely could count on getting the maximum a property could yield. The terms were usually a five-year lease at a fixed cash rental. Under such an inflexible arrangement, one year of bad crops inevitably put the tenants into arrears, once behind they rarely caught up, and the landlord found himself constantly lowering the rent. Sharecropping instead of cash provided the flexibility needed, but, as Pliny mentions in another letter, it involved constant surveillance of the tenants by inspectors to make sure there was no cheating. In any event, a tenant understandably had no interest in improving the property, particularly when he held so short a lease.

The alternative was slave labor, and a good many Roman farms, certainly most of the large ones, were run this way. It provided a more lucrative return than renting to tenants, but only at the cost of unflagging supervision and, when necessary, ruthlessness. The slaves were generally divided into two groups, those who were tractable enough to be left unguarded and those who had to be kept shackled. During the day these worked in chain gangs; at night they were locked up, still fettered, in *ergastula,* "work-houses," underground cellars lighted only by slits in the walls high enough to be out of reach. Roman writers on farming make it clear that all the slaves, fettered or unfettered, were viewed as so much livestock: they were well fed and kept healthy because this way they paid off best. Baths were available, but they were allowed to use them only on holidays, since the theory was that bathing was debilitating. They were encouraged to breed, because the children could either be raised as replacements or sold at a good price. Columella, who in the middle of the first century A.D. wrote a book on agriculture that is our best source of information, explains that his principle was to reward a mother of three with reduced work assignments and a mother of four with freedom. Bad as this sounds, things had at least improved since the second century B.C., when Cato the Elder advised selling off overage slaves the way one sold off oxen too old for the plow.

On any farm run by slave labor the key to success was the *vilicus,* the bailiff or farm manager, himself a slave but of higher quality than the others and trained for the job. Only an intelligent and energetic manager could get the work out of the help that would enable a property to produce the revenue it should. Over the manager was the agent, often a freedman, who was responsible for supervising the total holdings of an area, who reviewed the records and reported to the owner during his periodic visits.

Such visits were essential. As Columella puts it, a prudent landowner should see for himself

whether the slaves in the workhouses are carefully fettered . . . and whether the manager has chained or released any without authorization, . . . should inquire not only of the inmates but also of the slaves not in shackles—who are more to be believed—whether they are getting what is their due, should sample the quality of their food and drink by tasting it himself, should check on their clothing, mittens, and foot coverings. What is more, he should give them frequent chances to register complaints against those who treat them cruelly or dishonestly.

There were still independent peasants around. Probably most were concentrated in the area of large towns and cities, specializing in vegetables for the local market; this could be done with good success as a family operation. Peasants who were not so conveniently located and raised traditional crops, such as grain or vines, could help make ends meet by hiring out to their wealthy neighbors at harvest or vintage time, when additional hands were needed. And they could always pick up extra money by taking on dangerous chores, since owners of slave-run farms preferred to hire men for such work rather than use their own people—exactly like plantation owners in the antebellum South who reckoned that the death of a day-laborer "merely increased the Kingdom of Heaven; if a slave were killed, there was $1,500 gone." There were very few Roman squires, owners of large farms who lived on them all year round and ran them in person. All in all, in Italy of the second century A.D. most crops and fruits were raised, most sheep and goats grazed, by tenants or slaves on estates that belonged to landlords in Rome or other big cities.

Italy has a Mediterranean climate with scant rainfall. The ancient farmer, like his modern counterpart, practiced dry farming, as it is called, in which the major concern is to preserve the moisture in the soil. In order to prevent its evaporation, he plowed his land at least three times a year or even more—nine times in the clayey terrain of Tuscany. He used the type of plow that merely breaks the ground, for exposing the earth too deeply would allow moisture to escape. He let fields lie fallow every other year—a system that did its part in driving the small farm out of existence, since it forced a family, with limited acreage to begin with, to live off the produce of only half of it. Vineyards were carefully hoed to reduce evaporation, and equally carefully weeded, since no intrusive growth was to usurp any of the precious moisture.

Though farms concentrated on grain or vines or olives, this was never to the exclusion of all else. There were almost always a vegetable patch, orchard, and barnyard, at least to serve the needs of the staff if not for market. The patch yielded just about the range of produce we have today. So did the orchards, despite the repeated statement that citrus fruits were unknown to the Romans. The wall paintings at Pompeii and Herculaneum include oranges, lemons, and limes, as well as apples, peaches, pears, plums, and so on. Nuts were walnuts, chestnuts, hazelnuts, and almonds. What did differ from its modern counterpart was the barnyard. Roman farms, particularly those that catered to big-city markets whose customers were looking for fowl more exotic than chicken, goose, or duck, raised guinea hens, pheasants, peacocks, and thrushes.

Most farms had at least some livestock. There were sheep and goats, partly for the clip to weave into clothes for the family or help, partly for the milk to make into cheese; often pigs, which could be fed cheaply on slops (herding pigs for market was concentrated in the north, where there were still oak forests and consequently acorns); and generally a limited number of cattle, more for the manure than anything else. And every farm kept bees, since honey was the ancient world's sugar.

Of the work animals, the most important were the yokes of oxen for pulling the plows. Horses were rarely used for farm work, being too expensive; they were bred to race and to provide mounts for the cavalry and the couriers in the government post. Carts were drawn by yokes of oxen or spans of mules, and the beast of burden was the donkey.

The tools used on a Roman farm are all familiar: plow, harrow, spade, mattock, hoe, rake, for turning the soil; scythe and sickle for reaping; flails for threshing, or a threshing board pulled by oxen (when the threshing was not done simply by having animals or men tread on the crop); winnowing fans for winnowing. A farmer from Neolithic times would have recognized most of them. As a matter of fact, aside from improved drainage and irrigation, certain better strains of seed and fruit, and the like, there had been precious little advance in agricultural technology since his day. Even so simple yet superbly useful a gadget as the wheelbarrow did not arrive on the scene until the thirteenth century, when it was borrowed from China. The most remarkable example of technological laggardness is the water mill. Rome had water mills at least by the first century B.C.; yet then and forever after, their use was limited to certain large-scale installations connected with the army. Though a water mill could grind in three minutes what took a man with a hand quern an hour, its possibilities were not exploited until the Middle Ages. The ancient landowner, for whatever reason—and many have been offered—sought what he considered a reasonable return; he never turned his mind toward ways to extract every penny he possibly could.

CHAPTER IV

In the City

"I found Rome a city of brick and left it one of marble," boasted Augustus, and his successors carried on in the same spirit. In the center, the broad hollow more or less ringed by the seven hills, the emperors raised or rebuilt the structures whose remains have drawn tourists for centuries: the forum, or public square, surrounded by the Hall of Records, the Senate House, law courts, temples; the new forums connected with it, with more law courts and temples, as well as colonnades for leisurely strolling; the impressive imperial palaces that crowned the hill flanking it; the vast public baths. Sumptuousness was the keynote also on the upper slopes and crowns of some of the hills, the Quirinal and Caelian and Aventine, the residential quarters favored by the rich. There was even a rural note, on the Esquiline Hill and the Pincian, where a few great potentates lived in mansions surrounded by spacious gardens. However, the moment one left these gilded neighborhoods and moved back toward town center along the depressions between the hills, the city of brick was still very much in evidence. Here were the middle- and lower-class quarters, marked by block after block of apartment houses, packed cheek by jowl to fill every available foot of space. Shops lined the street level, and above them rose three, four, or sometimes even more stories of flats.

Let us follow the denizens of the various quarters in their daily rounds.

First, a well-to-do couple ensconced in a handsome private house, a replica, more or less, of those uncovered in Pompeii (page 67 below). The ancients, with only oil lamps for artificial light, lived between dawn and dusk. As a matter of fact, their way of telling time was to divide this period into twelve hours, even though it meant that from season to season the hours varied in length: on December 21, for example, with dawn about 7:30 A.M. and dusk 4:30, the hours were only forty-five minutes long; in midsummer, with dawn about 4:30 and dusk 7:30, they were seventy-five minutes. The well-to-do, unless they belonged to the ancient jet set, whose members turned night into day and vice versa, rose at dawn along with everybody else, that is, between 4:30 and 7:30 A.M. depending on the time of year. There was no great incentive to linger in bed, since Roman bedchambers were for sleeping, not passing time. Even in a rich man's home they were mere cubicles (the very word comes from their Latin name—*cubiculum*), with never more than a small window and often none. Window glass was not used, only shutters; so during cool weather one either kept them closed and stayed in the dark or opened them and shivered. The furniture was minimal: aside from the bed, just a chair, perhaps a chest, and the inevitable chamber pot.

The morning toilette for the master of the house was simple and quick. As was the universal ancient practice, he had slept in his under-clothes—a light sleeveless knee-length tunic and under it a loincloth, which functioned as undershorts. It took him but a moment to slip on his sandals, dash some cold water over his face—no more was required, since he was sure to go to the barber and the baths later—and if his day included a formal morning call or a session in the Senate or law courts or the like, put on his toga. This might cause some delay: it was no easy job to get this clumsy white robe, round in shape and three yards in diameter, to fall in the proper folds. His valet, an able and quick-witted slave, helped him arrange it, brought him his bite of breakfast, and he was ready for his day.

The lady of the house needed somewhat more time. Usually she had her own room. She too slept in her underclothes—loincloth, brassiere, and a light tunic that was a sort of shift (Martial has some cutting lines about a frigid wife, presumably literally as well as figuratively, who used to go to bed fully clothed). What could not be hurried was her hairdo, for the fashion in vogue in much of this period called for mountainlike tiers of curls. The *ornatrix,* the slave girl who did the mistress's hair and made her up, had no easy job, particularly if the lady of the house was fussy or irascible or both. Make-up involved chalk or white lead on the brow, ashes or powdered antimony for eye shadow, red lead or various plant dyes for rouge and lipstick. The mistress was then draped in her *stola,* the distinctive garment of a Roman matron, a graceful tunic that fell to her feet, and over this, when ready to go out of doors, she wrapped her *pallium,* or cloak. Even conservative matrons who wore the traditional white *stola* went in for colors in the *pallium*—red, violet, yellow, blue, or combinations. Their less inhibited sisters wore colored *stolae* as well, at times touched up with embroidery or decorations in the weave.

A wife, unless she joined her husband in a morning call, would spend the early hours at home issuing instructions to her staff of slaves and making sure they carried them out. Housekeeping was relatively simple, since there were no carpets to pick up dirt and scant furniture to move about. Floors, of mosaic or concrete, were left uncovered, and aside from the dining room with its couches and table, there was elsewhere little more than chairs, stools, benches, small tables, and lampstands to hold clusters of oil lamps. Rather than elegant furnishings, Romans preferred to adorn their homes with masterpieces of Greek art, with copies of famous paintings frescoed on the walls, and bronze or stone replicas of famous statues in niches, corners, and along colonnades. Probably the most burdensome housework chores were emptying the ashes from the charcoal braziers, which supplied the only heat, cleaning the oil lamps, and hauling water and wastes.

A select circle of the high and mighty remained at home in the early morning to receive formal calls; on these occasions the horde of lesser folk who lived off their patronage hurried to pay their respects—and at the same time press for favors they had to ask, pass on useful information they might have garnered, receive confidential instructions, or merely show their face (on occasion their wife's face as well). In return they were given a modest handout in food or money; this daily tipping of their retinue by the high and mighty was a standard feature of upper-class life in Rome.

By the third hour—9 A.M. in winter and 7 in summer—the well-to-do were at their occupations. A notable who was a member of the Senate might be attending one of the sessions. Another might be at the law courts, either as party to or pleading a case. One of the many who were *rentiers* might have returned home to consult with his accountant, a highly trained and trusted slave, or dictate correspondence to a secretary, yet another skilled slave.

By noon their day's work was done. They joined their wives for a light lunch, had a siesta, and then probably headed for the barbershop to be shaved. This was a leisurely procedure, during which one chatted with the other customers, passing on the day's gossip; in an age that used neither shaving soaps nor creams but only hot water, it could also be a painful one. About the eighth or ninth hour—12:30 to 1:30 in winter, two hours later in summer—they joined the throngs heading for the nearest public bath, all save the few wealthy enough to have a private set of baths at home. Here they started out with some exercise: the athletic-minded heaved at weights or worked out with dumbbells or wrestled; the less serious played ball—the young ones strenuous games with a small hard ball, the elderly a decorous tossing back and forth of a medicine ball. This was followed by an anointing with oil and what we would call a Turkish bath, generally ending with a cold plunge. From the baths they headed back home to don dinner clothes, the *cenatoria,* "dinner suit," a light, comfortable tunic of particularly bright colors. Wives too would exchange their *stolae* for a female version of the garment. Dining would last until dusk or past it, and by then it was time to go to bed.

The middle class, since they lived in apartments, had no room for a corps of household slaves: the master did without a valet, and the mistress probably had the maid of all work double as *ornatrix*. If the master was a native-born Roman, living in shabby gentility off his connection with one of the great, he put on a toga and hustled out at the crack of dawn to pay the mandatory morning call. If he was a freedman, or the descendant of freedmen, he dispensed with the toga and donned a street-going tunic, with a cloak over it if the weather was cool, and strode off to the workshop, store, auction ground, warehouse, or whatever, where he earned his living. The poor man, a poverty-stricken freeman or freedman, or a slave living in his own quarters, was of course up at dawn and was out of the house in a twinkling, since he had slept in the clothes he wore by day and all he had to do was lace on his sandals and pull his cloak off the bed, where it had been doubling as a blanket. Both tunic and cloak were dark, either of dark wool or dyed a dark color; white showed the dirt, and cleaning was expensive. His day did not end at noon, since workshops and stores stayed open till dusk or later in winter; the shops along the main streets of Pompeii all had lamps on their fronts to illuminate them after dark. He, no less than his betters, ended up at the public baths, but because of his longer working day he arrived a good hour or more after they had.

Businessmen and workers put in not only a full day but a full week. There was no regular day of rest to look forward to; Sunday became such only in A.D. 321, after Constantine officially accepted Christianity. The Roman calendar in the second century A.D. included some 135 days in which religious festivals were celebrated or the government held official games, but these were in no sense public holidays during which everyone dropped his tools or closed shop. No doubt when the games were on, many a craftsman or tradesman knocked off work to spend some time watching the gladiators or chariots, but the only days that guaranteed a man repose were the festivals celebrated by his craft. March 19 somehow came to be sacred to Minerva and was taken off by doctors, cleaners, dyers, and, to the great joy of schoolchildren, teachers. On May 15 merchants honored their patron god Mercury; on June 7 the Tiber fishermen celebrated their own games; on June 9, when women honored Vesta, bakers for some reason took a holiday too; on July 23 and August 17 barge handlers and dockhands honored Neptune and Portunus (god of harbors) respectively, and so on. All slaves, as we have seen, had the Saturnalia off and, hard on its heels, a festival called the Compitalia. Some apprenticeship contracts have survived, and these indicate that on the average there were no more than thirty to forty nonworking days in the course of a year.

The millionaires who lived in the mansions on the Quirinal or Esquiline were originally aristocrats, members of Rome's ancient families whose income came from their landholdings supplemented by some high-level moneylending. The noble Brutus once made a loan to a Greek community that was hard put to pay its taxes, at an interest rate of 48 percent. Crassus, whose fortune helped finance Caesar's political career, made part of it by snapping up real-estate bargains; he had scouts constantly on the lookout for fires, would arrive hastily on the scene as soon as one was reported, and would offer a knock-down price to the agonized owner. However, two centuries of life under the empire changed considerably the complexion of the wealthy class. It now included men of lesser families, even of humble origin, who, by taking advantage of the opportunities offered in Rome's burgeoning economy, made their pile—and spent it conspicuously. Some became rich in government service. Narcissus and Pallas, for example, two Greeks who started as slaves in the imperial service, rose to become secretary of state and the treasury respectively under Claudius and Nero; in the process, the first accumulated a fortune of 400 million sesterces (some $1.6 billion) and an elegant house on the Quirinal, the second a fortune of 300 million sesterces and a garden estate on the Esquiline. Some made their money through commerce, like Trimalchio, Petronius's hero, a Greek ex-slave who boasts of how he got his start when he put what money he had into "a cargo of wine, added bacon, beans, perfumes, a load of slaves . . . and netted a cool 10,000,000 on that one voyage."

The middle class, on the other hand, reversed the ethnic mix: it included a relatively small number of citizens of Roman ancestry and a large number of freedmen of foreign origin whose rise, though it stopped far short of Trimalchio's dizzy heights, enabled them to live comfortably in a roomy apartment in a good neighborhood with an appropriate staff of household slaves. The native Roman was not at home in trade or commerce, which had always been the work of slaves or freedmen or provincials; this engendered the attitude that these occupations were beneath his dignity. If he could not be a *rentier*, he was willing to live off the daily handout from some grandee and the dole that every citizen resident in Rome was entitled to. Quick-witted freedmen, with their experience as slave accountants, managers, and secretaries to help them forward and no prejudices to hold them back, were not slow in stepping into the gap, and as the city grew they gradually took over the spectrum of activities needed to keep it going: they built its houses and monuments, baked its bread, jobbed its wine and meat and vegetables, buried its dead, ran its shops, restaurants, inns, brothels. They filled the ranks of the professions too, although this was not where the money was. Martial cautions a father not to make his son a lawyer or teacher:

> He wants an art that'll make him rich?
> A musician—there's the right career.
> Of if the boy seems not too bright,
> the building trade or auctioneer.

Teaching, medicine, the law—in Roman times these professions, with certain exceptions, brought scant return or prestige. The average primary- or secondary-school teacher barely stayed alive on the fees he collected from his students—when he was able to collect. Wealthy families had their own doctors, highly trained slaves or freedmen, almost always Greek. Greek also, either immigrants or freedmen, were the general practitioners who made calls in the Roman apartment

houses. They learned their art by going the rounds with some established doctor and assisting him—and the fact that six months of this sort
of internship was sometimes considered sufficient speaks volumes. The
lawyers fell into several groups. At the top of the profession was a select
circle of Roman noblemen who had taken up the study of the law as an
intellectual pastime; their learned opinions formed the basis of the
magnificent code that is one of Rome's great gifts to Western civilization. Then there were high-level barristers, like Cicero or his rival
Hortensius or Pliny the Younger, who argued cases involving governors and senators and who received handsome gifts as their reward since
they were not permitted to charge fees. And then there were the rank
and file, the Roman equivalents of ambulance chasers, ready to take any
kind of case they could, even to represent a rustic client who had no
cash and would pay with a basket of eggs or a sack of wheat. When
these fellows in court tried to add a bit of flair, to use some of the things
they had learned in law school, their down-to-earth clients quickly
called them to heel, as Martial testifies:

> Not poison, murder, or felonious assault,
>   but because a neighbor stole from me
> three she-goats, that's why I'm here in court.
>   And the judge insists you prove this, see?
> So why the orating, gestures, outcries,
>   on Hannibal's slitting of Roman throats,
> on Marius, Sulla, Carthage's lies?
>   Now you get going on my three goats!

There was no public transport of any kind in ancient Rome, which
explains why it became a city of densely packed apartment houses.
Only the rich, leading a life of leisure, could dwell away on the upper
slopes and summits of the hills. Working people had to be accommodated in the limited area within walking distance of the markets and
complex of government buildings at the center. The sole solution was
the apartment house, and as the population increased, these grew ever
taller and closer together. Very few remains have been found in Rome

itself, but we can get a fair idea of what they must have looked like from the blocks of flats uncovered at Ostia. Since demand constantly outran supply, apartments were scarce and expensive; landlords were even able to rent out, to those who could afford no better, the dark holes under staircases, cellars totally underground, and tiny garrets under the eaves—in some cases a climb of seven stories and never less than three or four.

The apartment-house dweller took in his stride such discomforts as the lack of heat, water, or sanitary facilities. However, there were two aspects of his existence that there was no getting used to—the threat of fire or collapse. Charcoal braziers and oil lamps were an ever-present hazard, and though the buildings themselves were of brick and coarse concrete, there was enough inflammable material about—wooden floor beams, rafters, and balconies, wood in the furniture, the spreads on the couches and beds—to set flames quickly racing through an entire house. Collapse was just as serious a menace. It took a long time before the emperors established building codes, and even after these were on the books, abuses were rampant. Speculative builders threw up shoddy tenements using poor materials, and as a result, the thunder of floors and walls giving way was all too often heard throughout the city, and wooden buttresses bracing enfeebled walls all too common a sight. Cicero himself was not above owning slum real estate of this kind; in a letter to a friend he reports that "two of my shop properties have collapsed and the rest are developing cracks. Not only the tenants but even the mice have cleared out."

A city of such size and dense population would have starved or perished in its own filth without the basic urban services. Thanks to the Romans' practical sense, gift at organization, and engineering skill, it had them—water supply, sewage, street maintenance and cleaning, fire and police departments, food supply, public recreation.

As one enters Rome today from the south, the remains of its aqueducts marching across the plain are still an impressive sight. In the second century A.D. there were ten of these mighty conduits. Running sometimes high above ground on arches and sometimes underground in tunnels, they carried in water from mountain springs and rivers as much as sixty miles away. Rome's water supply was one of its glories; and it is the one city service we know something about, for a stolid, matter-of-fact description written by Frontinus, who was commissioner of aqueducts under Nerva, has survived. The water was brought to public baths, public fountains—there were at least six hundred of these—and other such dispersal points. It was also piped into the houses of those lucky few who had official authorization for the privilege from the emperor. But running water in one's own home was so desirable an amenity that landlords were constantly bribing the employees of the service to tap the aqueducts for a water main to their houses. Eventually this draining off of water would significantly reduce the amount arriving at the outlet, and the emperor or commissioner would crack the whip and clean out the welter of illegal pipes.

The city, thus, had no problem so far as drinking or washing was concerned. And it was assured of a full belly, thanks to an arm of the government, created by Augustus, that arranged for, supervised, and distributed the supply of grain, which amounted to upwards of 135,000 tons annually. A certain amount went to the free market for sale to bakers, and a certain amount was retained from which the government issued to resident citizens, rich or poor, a monthly ration of free wheat—the "bread" of the "bread and circuses" that the Roman emperors provided to keep the populace content and thereby avoid civil disorder.

Other urban services were not quite as effective as water and food supply. Sanitation, for example, had some serious lacks. There was a good enough system of sewers to carry off rainwater, water from the public baths, and other waste waters. There were public latrines in all the bath complexes and spotted about the streets—an absolute necessity in a city where only private homes or ground-floor flats had facilities of their own. The latrines were first-class: they had handsome and durable marble seats, were flushed by a constant stream of running water, and were even heated, considerably sparing the users the chill of cold stone during the winter months. A commission existed to "repair, pave, and maintain streets." Unfortunately its functions did not include house-to-house garbage collection, and this led to indiscriminate dumping of refuse, even the heedless tossing of it out of windows. "Think . . . of the number of times," says Juvenal, "cracked or broken pots fall out of windows, of the amount of weight they bring down with a crash onto the street and dent the pavement. Anyone who goes out to dinner without making a will, is a fool . . . you can suffer as many deaths as there are open windows to pass under. So send up a prayer that people will be content with just emptying out their slop bowls!" There is a long section in the corpus of Roman law given over to causes for action "against those who pour or throw anything on passersby," which goes into all the niceties of liability (for example, if a slave did the dumping, who was liable, he or his master? If a guest, he or the host?).

One of Augustus's most welcome innovations was to give Rome its first fire and police departments. For policing the city during the daylight hours, he established a corps of three thousand men, organized on military lines and sharing the barracks of the emperor's special guard; subsequent emperors increased the number. The fire department took care of whatever policing was done at night—not very much, as we shall see in a moment. This was a body of seven thousand recruited from freedmen. They were not all housed in one barracks, but in seven main stations and fourteen branch stations strategically placed throughout the city. Each station had its staff of specialists: pump and water handlers; "hookers," who presumably used their instruments as modern firemen do; "blanketers," that is, men with blankets soaked in vinegar for smothering flames; catapultists for knocking down walls; and "mattress men," perhaps for catching people jumping from the upper stories. Each station also had four doctors for administering first aid to the staff or victims. Part of the personnel stayed at the ready in the stations, and part, equipped with buckets of water and axes, made the rounds of the city all night long. The intent was to catch a fire just as quickly as possible because, without modern pumps to bring water to the upper stories, there was no stopping it once it had taken hold.

Lastly, we come to public recreation. Here we again discern the

Roman Wine Shop. A customer holds up his own jug under a spout that passes through the counter. The wine seller pours through the spout from a jug of the requested capacity. Above his head hang jugs of varying capacities arranged in order of size. Archaeological Museum, Dijon.

Roman genius for building and organizing. If the people of Rome had to sardine themselves into waterless and airless chambers for the night, they at least were able to prelude this by washing and relaxing in public facilities that have never been outdone for size and splendor. The public baths erected by the emperors were vast structures, the biggest covering the equivalent of several city blocks, and the opportunity for a complete Turkish bath—warm room, hot room, sweat room, followed or preceded by a cold plunge—was only one of the amenities they offered. The bathing area occupied the center of the complex; surrounding it were gardens with paths for walking, exercise courts, meeting rooms, recital and lecture halls, shops where massages or beauty treatments were to be had. One could easily while away the better part of an afternoon there, watching the games being played, chatting with friends, listening to recitations, buying a snack or drink from the vendors who circulated about, as well as bathing. Augustus's great minister Agrippa built the first of the imperial public baths sometime before 19 B.C. The next was contributed by Nero, a gorgeous structure on which he spared no expense; as Martial quipped, "What worse than Nero? What better than his baths?" One of the greatest of them dates from just after the period that particularly concerns us, the Baths of Caracalla, so enormous that Rome's current summer opera performances, including productions of *Aïda* that call for camels, chariots, and horses, as well as an army of supers, are staged in the ruins of what was once the hot room.

The public baths provided some area for strolling. There was still more in the new forums the emperors built off the original one, in various porticoes they erected, and in a number of public gardens, including some that once belonged to Julius Caesar and that he donated to the people of Rome. For the intellectually minded there were public libraries. Users could take books out or read them there—although the ancient way of reading, aloud and not silently, might have created problems on a busy day. And then there were the nearest things to museums that the ancient world offered, temples that had, by virtue of various dedications, become repositories of art and other cherished objects. During Rome's centuries of conquest its generals plundered ruthlessly, and they brought back art by the cartload to adorn their capital.

There was one important form of recreation that the denizens supplied for themselves—social clubs. These were a universal feature of the Roman world, to be found in small towns as well as major centers. Usually they were organized according to business or trade, running the gamut from, say, the Shipowners Association, whose members were all substantial businessmen who were able to elect even an emperor as their honorary patron, to humble organizations of stevedores or other manual laborers whose membership was totally slave. They were in no sense guilds or unions; their prime function was to serve as social clubs and burial societies, to maintain quarters where the members could hold banquets on fixed occasions or merely get together whenever they had free time, and to enable members to build up a fund to ensure they got decent burial when they died. Here, for example, is part of the bylaws of a humble group that calls itself the Association of Diana (the goddess) and Antinoüs (the deified favorite of Hadrian):

It was voted unanimously that whoever desires to enter this society shall pay an initiation fee of 100 sesterces [$400] and an amphora of good wine, and shall pay his monthly dues of 5 *asses* [about $5]. It was voted further that, if anyone has not paid his dues for six consecutive months and the common lot of mankind befalls him, his claim to burial shall not be considered, even if he has provided for it in his will. It was voted further that upon the decease of a paid-up member of our body there will be deducted a funeral fee of 50 sesterces to be distributed at the pyre [among those attending]; the obsequies, furthermore, will be performed on foot. . . .

It was voted further that if any slave member of this society becomes free, he is required to donate an amphora of good wine. . . .

Masters of the dinners, appointed four at a time in turn in the order of the membership list, shall be required to provide an amphora of good wine each, and for as many members as the society has bread costing 2 *asses,* sardines to the number of four, a setting, and warm water with service. . . .

It was voted further that if any member desires to make any complaint or bring up any business, he is to bring it up at a business meeting, so that we may banquet in peace and good cheer on festive days.

It was voted further that any member who moves from one place to another [at a banquet] so as to cause a disturbance shall be fined 4 sesterces. Any member, moreover, who speaks abusively of another or causes an uproar shall be fined 12 sesterces. Any member who uses abusive or insolent language to a president at a banquet shall be fined 20 sesterces. . . .

From the excavations at Ostia we get a good idea of what the headquarters of a rich society looked like, with inner gardens, colonnades, elegant dining rooms and salons, a multitude of small chambers. The likes of the Association of Diana and Antinoüs must have been satisfied with whatever bare hall or cellar they could afford. Sometimes these lowly groups were lucky enough to convince the prominent businessman whom they had honored with election as patron to show his gratitude by standing the expense of a clubhouse.

Water, free bread, promenades, the baths, private clubs—these went a long way toward brightening the days of the Roman apartment-house dweller. What darkened them were the same factors that darken life in so many cities of today: Rome was overcrowded, noisy, and violent.

The apartment houses lined streets that were twisted and narrow. The whole of the great city had no more than a half dozen of what we would call main avenues, and these rarely were wider than twenty to twenty-five feet. Lesser avenues were twelve to sixteen feet, and side streets a mere six. Hardly any, main or minor, ran in a straight line; most wound about exactly as in the older parts of Rome today. And those that mounted the slopes of the seven hills were not only narrow but steep. In the populous quarters, all streets were forever in shadow because of the towering buildings on both sides and forever jammed because of their scanty width. Julius Caesar faced up to the situation and passed a law banning all wheeled vehicles from dawn to dusk; the only exceptions were the carts that carried in materials for the erection of public buildings and carried out debris from demolitions connected with these, and the carts that hauled away the refuse of the street cleaners. The law was enforced for centuries and applied in all the other cities of Italy, not merely Rome. But this did not solve the problem of pedestrian traffic. "I hurry," says Juvenal, "but there's a wave ahead of me in the way, and the crowd is so dense the people behind jam against my back and sides. Someone rams me with his elbow, someone else with a pole, this fellow cracks my head with a two-by-four, that one with a ten-gallon jug, my shins are thick with mud, now I'm being trampled by somebody's big feet—and there goes a soldier's hobnail in my toe!" Not only were the streets narrow to begin with, but shopkeepers used to spill out into them to gain additional room, which reduced the free passage even further—pedestrians had to squeeze past butchers chopping on their blocks, barbers shaving customers in the chair, sausage-sellers grilling their wares, and—just as in modern Rome—the tables of the neighborhood restaurants and bars.

Then there was the noise. Since the apartments were small and uncomfortable, Romans spent most of their waking hours in the streets, the way they do in the older parts of the city today. From dawn to dusk there was a babble of voices, of shopkeepers and peddlers hawking, of beggars whining, of schoolchildren chanting their lessons, of people just passing the time of day. Add to that the din that came from the artisans' shops, the incessant tapping of coppersmiths, the heavy pounding of blacksmiths, the sawing and hammering of carpenters, the chiseling of stonecutters, and so on. The racket along certain streets must have been infernal. Nor did night bring any surcease, thanks to the banning of traffic during the day; that was when one began to hear the tramping of hooves, the cracking of whips, the swearing of teamsters, the creaking of carts, and the tortured squealing of their wheels—which alone would awake the dead, since the only lubricants known were animal fat and the lees of olive oil, and there was never very much of either to spare. As Juvenal observed, "It takes a lot of money to get a night's sleep in Rome."

When dusk fell, the rank and file secured themselves behind bolts and bars until dawn. For there was no street lighting in ancient Rome, and only those who could afford a retinue of slaves to light up the way with torches and to serve as bodyguard dared walk about in the dark. To go out alone was an invitation to be mugged. "Here is the prelude to the fighting," explains Juvenal,

if it's fighting when he does all the punching and all you do is get hit. He stands in your way and orders you to stop, and you've got to obey; what can you do when you're being forced by someone raging mad and, what's more, stronger than you are? "Where are you from?" he hollers, "whose beans and rotgut have you filled your belly with . . . ? So you won't talk? You talk or get a kick in your rear. . . . " It makes no difference whether you try to say something or retreat without a word, they beat you up all the same. . . . You know what the poor man's freedom amounts to? The freedom, after being punched and pounded to pieces, to beg and implore that he be allowed to go home with a few teeth left.

Things must have improved somewhat with the introduction of street lighting, but this did not take place until the fourth century A.D.

If ancient cities eventually achieved street lighting, there are two other simple yet immensely useful municipal services that they never achieved at all—the comprehensive naming of streets with the posting of these names on signs, and the numbering of houses. To be sure, certain Roman streets did have names. We know that what is today the Corso was in ancient times the Via Lata, "Broadway," that what is today the lower part of Via Cavour was the Argiletum, the main avenue through one of Rome's most crowded quarters. There were streets named after the activities concentrated on them (Vicus Sandalarius, "Street of the Sandal Makers," Vicus Argentarius, "Street of the Money-Changers"); after a monument nearby or to which they led (Vicus Apollinis, "Apollo Street," after the Temple of Apollo nearby, Vicus Portae Collinae, "Street of the Porta Collina," since it led to that gate); after the inhabitants (Vicus Patricius, "Patrician Street," Vicus Tuscus, "Etruscan Street"). But others bore no names at all, and none bore street signs. And the numbering of houses simply did not exist. As a consequence, in ancient Rome one gave directions thus:

You know that house there, the one that belongs to Cratinus, the millionaire? Well, when you get past that house, go straight down the street there to the left, then when you get to the temple of Diana go right. Then just before you get to the town gate, right by a watering pond there, you'll find a little bakery and, opposite it, a carpenter's shop. That's where he is.

Or a person would say, "He told me it was the seventh building from the town gate." On letters one simply put down the name of the recipient, never an address. And on dog collars, all one could do was inscribe: "Return me to the house of Elpidius on the Caelian Hill."

CHAPTER V

A Roman Gentleman

He helped ladies with their financial problems and advised them on family matters. He wrote letters of recommendation for his friends' children and used his influence in their behalf. He worried over the health of his household staff, even sending them overseas for a cure when he felt they needed it. He subscribed to the spectrum of worthwhile charities. He attended every literary occasion and considered it his duty to encourage promising talent (he had, of course, his own definition of "promising"). He was an ornament to the bar, at his proudest when, clad in a pure white, elegantly draped toga—the Roman equivalent of the barrister's wig and gown—he held jurors and audience spellbound as he pressed a client's suit with telling phrases. Transfer him from the first to the nineteenth century, and from Rome to Boston, and Pliny the Younger would make an ideal hero for a novel by J. P. Marquand.

We know hardly anything about the private lives of most figures from the ancient world. For writers there are only the scraps of information to be gleaned from their works, for historical personages the statements made by friends, enemies, or scandalmongers. Pliny is one of a handful of exceptions, because we have the letters he wrote to his cir-

cle of friends; he meticulously saved copies and published them. They
are not all intimate missives hot from the pen, like Cicero's, which
race along in colloquial language and, as informal letters will, leap from
point to point, from burning issues of the day to the most trivial private
matters. Pliny wrote his with the thought of publication in mind: he
polished every sentence until it glistened, and he almost sounds at times
as if he felt posterity were glancing over his shoulder as he sat with his
pen and tablets. But the letters are no less revealing for all that. They
reflect unerringly the image of an eminently proper Roman, ready to
raise an eyebrow at the slightest breach of decorum, always striving to
be *comme il faut,* utterly lacking in fresh or original ideas, yet at the same
time the kind of man the world may be thankful exists, one dedicated to
the old-fashioned ideal of public service, intelligent and understanding,
far readier with praise than censure, decent to the core. Had you been
invited to dinner with the Plinys, you would have groaned—but taken
advantage of the occasion to ask him to be executor of your will.

Pliny was born in A.D. 61 or 62. His father died when he was young,
and he was adopted by his uncle, his mother's brother, Pliny the Elder,
an eccentric gentleman who spent every crumb of time he could spare
from an active career as public servant in the research that enabled him
to compile the enormous one-man encyclopedia that has made his
fame; one of his nephew's best-known letters tells how he died when
his eager curiosity led him to take too close a look at Vesuvius during
the fatal eruption that buried Pompeii. Young Pliny, as one would
expect, was a model child, dutiful, hard-working, earnest, and preco-
cious—at age fourteen he had written a Greek tragedy, which years
later he was not quite ready to admit was all bad. The son of a rich and
eminent family, he was tutored at home, and he admired and respected
his teacher. University education in his day was almost wholly devoted
to the study and practice of public speaking—how to make political
orations, how to address a court. Pliny took his at Rome under none
other than the renowned Quintilian, the John Dewey of Roman education. He then embarked on the standard career of a responsible Roman aristocrat, a lifetime devoted to public service. After a stint in the

army—he served as lieutenant with a unit stationed in Syria—he began a steady climb up the rungs of the political ladder, achieving in A.D. 100, when not yet forty, the office of consul, or titular head of state. Both before and after he filled certain posts that the emperors, well aware of his sense of responsibility and capacity, entrusted him with. Whether it was as commissioner of sewers for Rome or governor of an important overseas province, he carried out his duties in exemplary fashion, with total dedication. But his true joy lay in his career as a barrister. Forensic oratory in his day was more than a matter of law, it was one of the highest forms of literary endeavor, and Pliny fancied himself first and foremost a literary man. He argued not only important cases involving property and inheritances in Rome's most prestigious court, but a number of *causes célèbres* in the Senate, in which he defended or prosecuted fellow members charged with malfeasance while serving as governors of overseas provinces. Pliny was proud as punch of the part he played in these, and why not?—he was able to hold forth for five hours at a clip with a captive audience that included the cream of Roman society right up to the emperor.

He was married three times. We know nothing of the first union, of the second only that his wife died, but a good deal about the third. It was with a much younger woman who worshipped him—or convinced him she did—as a literary giant. In a letter to her aunt, he reports gratifiedly how she reads every word he writes, listens to every public recitation he makes, chants his poetry, composing her own musical accompaniment on the lyre, and follows his pleadings in court so anxiously that she has couriers on hand in the audience to race back with word of favorable reactions, outbreaks of applause, and the verdict. Pliny, who shared her opinion of his literary merits, adored her. His one sorrow was that, through her girlish ignorance, she neglected to take some appropriate precautions and so brought on a miscarriage that forever prevented her from having children. He was sorely disappointed, for he wanted offspring to carry on the family name and tradition of public service, but it was the sole sadness this paragon of feminine dutifulness (or shrewdness) ever caused him.

Pliny's birthplace was Como, on the lake, where the family owned considerable property. He moved to Rome in his teens for his higher education and stayed there to carry on his career in politics and at the bar. He had a house in the fashionable district on the Esquiline Hill and passed his days like most Roman gentlemen of the time: up at dawn to make or receive calls, then off to the Senate, the courts, or any of the myriad chores that fell a busy and important man's way. "If you ask someone," he writes to a friend, " 'What did you do today?,' he'll tell you, 'I was at a boy's coming-of-age ceremony or a betrothal or a marriage, one fellow asked me to witness a will, another to stand by him in court, another to advise him in rendering verdicts. . . . ' " To all this Pliny added punctual, dutiful, and never-failing attendance at literary recitations. These played in the cultural life of the city the role that musical recitals or art shows do today. The literary lions read their poems or orations or essays or whatever in the elegance of a rich friend's salon; the threadbare writer on the make spent his last penny to hire some barren hall. The sessions invariably went on for hours and not uncommonly for days. Pliny spent three whole days listening to the poems of one of his long-winded literary friends—and took three himself to read *in toto* a panegyric he had composed on the emperor Trajan. Pliny spelled literature with a capital *L* and believed it was to be supported at all cost, so whatever recitations were going on were sure to find him in the audience, listening attentively and directing killing looks at those who sauntered in late or ostentatiously left before the reading was over or, worst of all, sat stony-faced without showing the least sign of appreciation. He was on intimate terms with all the well-known literary figures. He collaborated with Tacitus, the historian, in conducting a celebrated prosecution in the Senate. Suetonius, the biographer of the Caesars, was a close friend, and Pliny was responsible for getting him political favors. Martial wrote a flattering piece comparing him with Cicero, and Pliny repaid with money for the journey when the poet left the city. To be accounted a literary light was his greatest pleasure, and he tells with gusto the story of how someone sitting next to Tacitus at the races, after some serious literary conversation, inquired

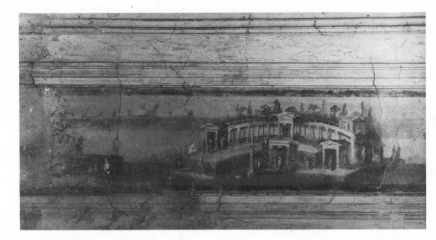

Seaside Villa. The building faces the sea. The rooms are shaded from the sun by a continuous portico along the front. Wall painting from Pompeii, first century A.D.

who his neighbor was, and when Tacitus replied, "You know me, of course, from your reading," asked, "Are you Tacitus or Pliny?"

It was de rigueur for all who belonged to the upper crust to escape periodically from the daily round in the city and relax in their country villas. Everybody of means boasted not merely one but several, in various attractive spots along the shore and in the mountains. Then there were the manor houses on the farms they owned for income; a visit to these enabled them to combine country air with business. Pliny had an elaborate seaside villa conveniently located not far from Ostia, near enough for him to be able to leave the city after a day's work and arrive before dusk; if he was not staying long enough to make it worthwhile to fire up his own set of baths in the villa, it was no trouble to run over and use commercial baths nearby. In a long letter he describes the place in detail, a charming, rambling complex whose rooms commanded lovely views of the sea. It had every kind of salon and chamber, including one study so secluded that Pliny was able to escape there even from the hullabaloo of the Saturnalia. His preferred summer villa was in the Tuscan hills. There the emphasis was on countering the heat rather than on pleasing vistas. The rooms, mostly on inner courts, were cool and dark, the walks were quiet and shaded, and day and night the sound that pervaded the place was the murmur of water, the plash of fountains. Pliny describes in detail how he used to spend his days there:

> I wake when I please, generally at dawn, often earlier, rarely later. I don't open the shutters, in the stillness and darkness being wonderfully removed from distractions. . . . I concentrate on what work I have on hand . . . then call my secretary and, letting in the daylight, dictate what I've composed. . . .
>
> About the fourth or fifth hour [8:30–10:30 A.M.]—there's no observing fixed times—I go to either the terrace or the covered portico, depending on the weather, think out, and dictate the rest. Then into my carriage, to continue concentrating just as when lying abed or walking . . . a short siesta, then a walk, and then I recite aloud a speech in Greek or Latin clearly and with emphasis, not so much for the sake of my voice as my digestion, though of course both are equally strengthened. Another walk, a rub-down with oil, exercise, and a bath. If I dine with my wife or a few people, we have a book read to us. After dinner, reading of a comedy or music. Then a walk about with my staff, some of whom are learned men. And so we pass the evening chattering on various topics. . . . Friends dropping in from the nearby towns take up part of my day; at times, when I'm feeling tired, the interruption is welcome and helps. Occasionally I go hunting—but with pen in hand, so that I come back with something even when I've bagged nothing!

Country life, however, was not always literary composition, strolling, and pleasant dinner parties. What made these activities possible, as well as the leisure in Rome to orate at the bar and in the Senate or to attend poetical declamations, was a substantial income, produced by the farmlands Pliny owned. The bulk of them were in the neighborhood of his birthplace, near Lake Como (the manor house in one was so close to the lake that Pliny could fish by dropping a line out of his bedroom window). Most were vineyards, and his practice was to let them out to tenants; the alternative, to farm them through slave labor, was repugnant to him: "I have no slaves in chains anywhere," he asserts categorically. But exploiting his properties gave him constant trouble. The tenants were forever falling so far in arrears that there was no chance of their ever catching up; he even decided, *faute de mieux,* to try sharecropping, a system that held little appeal for him. When the middlemen who had bought his grape crop on the vine discovered that things were turning out badly, Pliny decided it would be wise to allow them substantial rebates. One thing, however, is clear: despite all the talk of business troubles, Pliny never lacked for money, never had to reduce his standard of living, and never was forced to sell off any of his lands.

Public service to Pliny meant generosity not only with his time but with his income as well: he contributed to every conceivable kind of charity. Once when he was visiting in Como, a friend dropped by with his son to pay his respects. "Do you go to school?" Pliny asked the boy.

"Oh, yes."

"Where?"

"At Milan."

"Why not here?" At this point the boy's father broke in to explain that there was no school available at Como. Pliny, who, as we know, was childless and hence acting altogether disinterestedly, offered at once to help with a matching grant: he would supply one-third of the funds needed to hire teachers if interested parents would supply the other two-thirds. He was ready, he explains, to assume the whole expense, but if he did, it would have to be done through the municipality and that always meant graft and nepotism; a parent-run school was a far better idea. His interest did not stop with providing money; he sent off a letter to his friend Tacitus to find out whether the historian had among his literary acquaintances any likely candidates for the potential faculty. The school was only one of a number of handsome charities in behalf of his home town. He established an endowment for the support of needy boys and girls consisting of land that produced a yearly revenue of 30,000 sesterces (about $120,000). He built both a set of baths and a public library and thoughtfully included endowments to cover the cost of their upkeep. He set up a fund of close to two million sesterces (about $8 million), the income from which was to maintain one hundred slaves he had freed, and at their death, to finance an annual memorial banquet in his name for all the townspeople. He built a temple for the village near his Tuscan estate, he rebuilt a shrine that happened to be on one of his properties—the list could go on and on.

And then, when he was of an age to settle down to the full enjoyment of his routine in city and country, he was called away from it: the emperor Trajan appointed him governor of the province of Bithynia on the south shore of the Black Sea with particular instructions to straighten out as best he could the finances of the principal cities; these, because of local extravagance and mismanagement, were sadly in need of supervision. And so, in the fall of A.D. 111 or perhaps a year or so earlier, Pliny set out for his new post. It is one of history's great pieces of luck that, in his precise and methodical manner, he preserved not only the letters he wrote to the emperor but the latter's replies; the correspondence gives us a fascinating glimpse into the operation of Roman government, the manifold responsibilities the central administration took upon itself, and the care it gave to their execution. At Nicomedia, the province's chief center, Pliny found things in a lamentable state: the city, he informs Trajan, had poured a fortune down the drain in building a new aqueduct that turned out to be faulty, still more in trying another; might he please have the services of one of the imperial engineers to help plan a proper one? The town exported marble, timber, and other products, but it was terribly expensive to haul these the sixty-odd miles to the port; might he please have the services of one of the imperial engineers to explore the possibility of digging a canal? A huge fire had recently wiped out part of the city; might he go ahead and have the town set up a fire department? Things were hardly better elsewhere. The theatre at Nicaea, though not yet completed, was already falling to pieces because of poor construction, while the new gymnasium, replacing one that had burned down, was equally ill-planned. At Claudiopolis a new bath complex was being built in so badly chosen a spot that whether its completion would be worthwhile was questionable; in the lovely town of Amastris an open sewer that ran alongside one of the main squares not only looked horrible but stank to high heaven; at Sinope an aqueduct was desperately needed, and so on. On top of all these problems was the behavior of an odd religious sect whose members politely but stubbornly refused to display appropriate religious deference to the image of the emperor and the statues of the gods; they assured him that

the sum and substance of their fault or error was that they were accustomed to meet on a fixed day before dawn and sing responsively a hymn to Christ as to a god, and to bind themselves by oath . . . not to commit fraud, theft, or adultery, not to falsify their trust, nor to refuse to return a trust when called upon to do so [apparently they were explaining to Pliny the Ten Commandments]. When this was over, it was their custom to depart and to assemble again to partake of food—but ordinary and innocent food. Even this, they affirmed, they had ceased to do after the edict by which, in compliance with your instructions, I had forbidden political associations. Accordingly, I judged it all the more necessary to find out what the truth was by torturing two female slaves who were called deaconesses. But I discovered nothing else but depraved, excessive superstition.

Orders were orders: Christians by their refusal to acknowledge the official deities fell into the category of a subversive association, and the governor had no alternative except to prosecute them.

The last letter we have from Pliny's pen is an apology to the emperor for having made an exception to the rule that only people on official business might use the carriages and inns of the government courier service: he had granted permission for their use to his wife, who had just heard of the death of her uncle and was desperately anxious to rush back to Rome to comfort her aunt. It is not likely that Pliny ever rejoined her there. We hear no more of him, and the probabilities are that he died while still in Bithynia, thousands of miles away from the people, places, and way of life he had immortalized.

CHAPTER VI

The Slave

"I was no bigger than this candlestick here when I came out of Asia Minor. . . . For fourteen years I was the master's little darling. The mistress' too. . . . The gods were on my side—I became the head of the household, I took over from that pea-brain of a master. Need I say more? He made me co-heir in his will, and I inherited a millionaire's estate." The speaker is Trimalchio, the character in Petronius's novel, *The Satyricon,* who made it from the rags of a slave to the riches of a billionaire.

A slave becoming a master's heir and inheriting an estate worth millions? It seems unbelievable. Not in the Roman world of the first century A.D., when Petronius wrote. He was, to be sure, a novelist and not a historian, but his portrait of Trimalchio is based on reality. Though the slave was at the opposite end of the social spectrum from the likes of Pliny, thanks to certain Roman attitudes and ways, avenues of upward mobility bridged the gap between these extremes, and there were many slaves who made it part way across and some who, like Trimalchio, made it all the way.

Slavery is as old as war: it arose when a winning side, instead of killing off all the losers, discovered it was advantageous to take some home and make slaves of them. It existed throughout the millennia during which the civilizations of Mesopotamia and Egypt dominated the ancient world, but within limits: the victims became nurses, maids, concubines, valets, gardeners, and the like. Then, around the beginning of the sixth century B.C., there was a fundamental change: the Greeks expanded slavery, basing their entire economy on it, and this continued for the thousand years during which first the Greeks and then the Romans ruled the Mediterranean world.

The tasks that involved sweat and drudgery inevitably fell to the lot of slaves: they labored in the damp and darkness of the mines; they hacked and chipped in the quarries; they toiled in the fields. But there also fell to them much white-collar work: they were the clerks, cashiers, bookkeepers of ancient Greece and Rome. And they manned not only the lower levels of such work but the upper as well. Banks were owned by wealthy Greek or Roman families, but the officers who were in charge of them could be slaves or freedmen. The ships and cargoes that crisscrossed the Mediterranean belonged to wealthy Greeks or Romans, but the crews, from the lowest deckhand right up through the captain, could be slaves. Absentee landlords of great estates were able to spend their time in leisurely pursuits because the running of the holdings that supplied their income was all in the hands of slave or freedman managers backed by a staff of slaves. Romans with cash to invest often put it in city real estate; the agents who let the apartments, collected the rents, and saw to the repairs were slaves.

The white-collar work of slaves included that of governments as well as of individuals: they were the clerks, cashiers, bookkeepers of cities and states. At Athens, for example, the official in charge of the navy was a citizen elected by his fellow citizens, but the assistants who kept track of the galleys in the slips, their condition, what gear they had or lacked, whether there were shortages of rowers, and all such details, were slaves. (Incidentally, the rowers of these galleys, whether of Greek navies or Roman, were *not* slaves, as is so commonly thought; they were free men. Every now or then, because of some desperate emergency, the

Slaves at Work. The relief pictures a tomb in the form of a Roman temple and the crane used in constructing it, a windlass turned by a group of slaves walking on a treadmill built into the windlass wheel. Second century A.D. Lateran Museum, Rome.

benches were opened to slaves—and those who served on them were rewarded with their freedom.)

Among the Romans, especially during the flourishing period of the Roman Empire under discussion, slaves enjoyed more and more chances to lead comfortable lives and at the same time move toward gaining their freedom. This came about because of a vast increase in these years in the size and complexity of businesses and of the government bureaucracies and with it a corresponding increase in the number of white-collar jobs. Since native Romans had no taste for trade or commerce (aside from investing in them) and took a dim view of the routine of desk work, they turned over the tasks involved to slaves, and, since they were generous in granting manumission, particularly to the slaves who worked in their offices and homes, the white-collar slave worker could be fairly sure of eventually gaining it. Moreover, manumission among the Romans brought with it a precious gift— citizenship. Thus the freedman stood politically higher than the multitudes of freeborn peoples who lived in the lands Rome had conquered and were only Roman subjects, not citizens, and hence were denied the vote, marriage with a Roman citizen, access to Roman courts, and other privileges.

Throughout the Roman Empire slaves staffed the offices of towns and cities, and in Rome itself they staffed all the ranks of the emperor's bureaucracy: they were the nation's civil service. Those who demonstrated satisfactory ability could expect manumission by the age of thirty to thirty-five; after manumission they would carry on their duties as freedmen.

The paths in the imperial administration led right to the very top, to posts that today would be held by department heads, even cabinet ministers. During Claudius's reign, Pallas, a freedman, served as his secretary of the treasury, and Narcissus, another freedman, as his secretary of state. Both used their position to line their pockets and both became so incredibly rich that, to quote Claudius's biographer, "Once, when Claudius was grumbling about the shortage of cash in the treasury, someone said—and it was no joke—'You'd have plenty if your two freedmen would take you in as a partner.' " Pallas's brother was the Felix who earned everlasting notoriety for throwing St. Paul into prison; he had risen from slavery to the governorship of Judaea. Though slaves, as mentioned above, were never used as rowers of galleys in the Roman navy, ex-slaves could be in charge of those galleys: under Claudius and Nero there are three instances of them serving as commanders of fleets. Presumably the duties called for administrative rather than naval expertise.

Members of the imperial civil service did not even have to wait till they were freed to acquire riches; they were able to do so while still slaves. A particularly striking example is a certain Musicus Scurranus, who, under Tiberius, was an official in the department of disbursements for the province of Gaul based at Lyons. He died during a stay at Rome, and he had along with him at the time, as we learn from the inscription on his tombstone, no less than sixteen slaves of his own: his personal doctor, his business agent, a major-domo, a valet, two cooks, two footmen, two men in charge of his silver plate, two chamberlains, three body servants, and a woman whose duties are not specified. And these were just the ones in the entourage; there must have been an army of others at home. Even imperial slaves in far lower levels than Scurranus could live the good life. When the emperor Julian arrived at the palace in Constantinople and summoned the palace barber for a haircut, the man appeared in such gorgeous garb that Julian cracked, "I sent for a barber, not the Chancellor of the Exchequer"; when Julian asked where the money came from, "a hefty (*grave*) annual salary," he was told, "plus a lot of profitable requests for favors."

Government service was not the only area that offered such opportunities for slaves. There were as many or more for those employed in the running of businesses or of great households, the sort of post that gave Trimalchio his start. Slaves in such positions who had managed to accumulate enough money to serve as investment capital could work not only for the master but with him: they could become his partner in trade, in the holding of real estate, and so on. Posts of this sort were so sure a way of getting ahead that free men with bleak prospects would sell themselves into slavery in order to qualify for them. The free man who was a Roman subject living in one of the conquered lands could figure that, by so doing, he would eventually earn manumission and, with it, the citizenship. As Petronius has one of Trimalchio's friends say, "My father was actually a king. Why am I only a freedman now? Because I handed myself into slavery of my own free will. I wanted to end up a Roman citizen, not a tribute paying subject."

What of women? There were numerous female slaves in any large household serving as maids, hairdressers, masseuses, seamstresses, nurses, and the like. Many earned manumission, but upward mobility was open to them only through their husbands. The exceptions are those women whose beauty or charm or intellect won them highly placed lovers. Cytheris, for example, originally a slave dancer, after gaining her freedom became the mistress of a Roman aristocrat who held her in such regard that he included her in his banquets—much to the outrage of Cicero, a stuffy snob, when he was a fellow diner: "My god," he wrote to a friend later, "I never thought *she* would be there!" She left this lover for Mark Antony, who treated her even more handsomely, assigning her his own litter with her own host of attendants. Nero as a young man was desperately in love with a freedwomen named Acte, who had come to Rome as a slave from Asia Minor, and he actually wanted to marry her. She remained his mistress throughout and was one of the very few—the others his two old nurses—who dared give his body decent burial after he was assassinated. Vespasian, when his wife died, promoted a freedwoman from mistress to concubine and "though an emperor, regarded her almost as his legal wife."

In urban areas, the locale of most business and government offices, manumission was so common that ex-slaves came to make up a high proportion of the Roman citizenry. Their ability to get ahead was such that, as a whole, they formed the nearest thing there was to a Roman middle class, while numerous individuals, the Trimalchios and the Scurranuses, rose even higher. In Roman imperial times the making of lavish public donations was expected of the rich. Hitherto the main contributors had been Roman aristocrats, the likes of Pliny; now they were joined by these self-made *nouveaux riches*, the freedmen, who spent their money openhandedly to gain public honors for themselves and public honors and offices for their sons. In a place like Ostia (see Chapter 7), a bustling commercial center and port, freedmen were at the heart of its society. A monument found there bears an inscription telling that it had been erected by a certain Lucius Fabius Eutychus and setting forth the highlights of his career and his son's. He began as a slave in the city's civil service, where he rose from official attendant to junior clerk to chief clerk. In the course of time he was manumitted, and he apparently went into the construction business, judging from his election to a term as president of the builder's association. He made enough money to set up a fund of 12,500 denarii (ca. $200,000) "from the interest on which, at 5%, every year on July 20, his birthday, 550 will be divided among the town councillors present in the forum before the aforementioned statue, and 37½ among the chief clerks, 12½ among the junior clerks, 25 among the official attendants." The statue is "aforementioned" in an earlier part of the inscription devoted to Eutychus's son: the family's money had enabled him to do very well indeed, for he served

as a coopted member of the town council, as priest of the Divinized Hadrian (during which term as priest he alone—the first to do so—out of his own pocket paid for public theatrical performances), as commissioner of markets. Him the illustrious order of the town councillors honored with a public funeral and, in recognition of all his affection and industry, decreed that an equestrian statue be erected for him in the forum at public expense.

In but two generations Eutychus's family had risen from slavery to the lofty honor of a statue in the center of town.

Throughout the empire ex-slaves like Eutychus moved steadily higher in Roman society, helping themselves upward by their money, by liberal expenditure on highly visible charity; treating the whole population to a banquet on the donor's birthday or picking up the bill for gladiatorial games were particular favorites.

One freedman, who was not very rich, used whatever money he had for a far higher goal. This was the father of the Roman poet Horace. He had been a slave in the civil service of the town of Venusia in southern Italy, a collector of taxes or other public dues. In due course he earned manumission, bought a small farm, and had a son. When the boy was of school age he gave up the farm and moved to Rome because he felt that the education available at Venusia was not good enough. At Rome he not only turned the boy over to proper teachers but watched over his upbringing with loving care. He did not live to see the spectacular result: Horace, son of an ex-slave, became the protégé of one of Augustus's ministers, was often in the company of the emperor himself, and achieved a fame that would be, to use his own words, "a monument more enduring than bronze." In but two generations the family had risen from slavery to literary immortality.

There were multitudes of Greek and Roman slaves—the gangs in the mines or on the vast ranches—who lived lives as hopeless and full of hardship as the slaves on the sugar plantations of Brazil or the cotton plantations in the American south. But in the days of the Roman Empire there were also many, a great many, who were able to escape from slavery and mount the steps of the social ladder, in some cases to the very top.

CHAPTER VII

Two Resurrected Cities

"For several days past, there had been tremors of the earth; not too alarming, since they are frequent in Campania. But that night they became so violent people had the feeling everything was not merely moving but overturning. . . . By dawn daylight was still faint, hard to make out. The buildings around us were shaking. Though we were in an open space, it was small; we were terrified, certain they were coming down on us. At that point we finally resolve to leave the town. . . . Once beyond the houses, we halt—strange, fearsome sights meet us: the carriages, which we had ordered out, though on absolutely level ground, were rolling back and forth. . . . We also saw the sea sucked back on itself, as if it had been forced back by the quaking of the earth. No question about it, it had receded from the shore and left quantities of sea creatures stranded on dry sand. On the landward side, a dreadful black cloud, split by jagged, quivering shafts of fiery exhalation, yawned wide to reveal long flaming shapes. . . . Soon the cloud came down to earth and enveloped the sea; it had already enveloped and hidden Capri and removed the promontory of Misenum from sight. . . . By now ash was falling, though as yet lightly. I look back: dense blackness was pressing from behind, it followed us, rolling over the land like a river in flood. . . . The fiery lights continued, some distance away, then darkness again, then again the ash, thick and heavy. . . . At last the darkness thinned and dispersed as if into smoke or mist. Then there was true daylight, the sun even shone, but pale and murky, as it does during an eclipse. We trembled at the sight that met us, of everything changed and piled high with ashes like snow." So wrote Pliny the Younger in answer to a request from his friend Tacitus for an account of the fatal days when Vesuvius erupted and smothered the towns on its flanks, including Herculaneum and Pompeii, under a blanket of ash. It took place on August 24, 25, and 26 in the year A.D. 79; Pliny, then a youth of about eighteen, happened to be staying at Cape Misenum, a mere twenty miles as the crow flies from the tip of the volcano.

Pompeii lay undisturbed and hidden under the ash, its very location forgotten, until the middle of the eighteenth century, when the first excavators—or, to put it more accurately, hunters of art treasures— began to burrow in its ruins. As always, there was both official and unofficial digging: the first was promoted by the Bourbon kings of Naples, the other went on clandestinely to feed the lucrative market for Pompeian *objets d'art* that arose once the news of the spectacular finds had spread over Europe. Sir William Hamilton, British envoy to the court of Naples, built up a superb collection, including prize pieces from both Pompeii and Herculaneum; he sold it to the British Museum for £8400, and rumor had it that this was the price he paid to win the *femme fatale* he married in 1791—and lost soon after, when she began her celebrated liaison with Admiral Horatio Nelson. In 1860 excavation started in earnest, on a large scale and in serious fashion; with minor interruptions it has continued ever since. The result has been the laying bare of an ancient site that is unique. The catastrophe struck the town in the midst of its normal routine, and the ash has preserved things just as they were when people dropped them to run for their lives; in some pathetic cases it has preserved the people as well, those who did not make it to safety. No other archaeological excavation illustrates so vividly the nature of daily life in the ancient world. It is from Pompeii that we know in detail how the Romans decorated their houses, what furniture they kept in them, what silverware they put on their tables and what cooking utensils on their hearths, what instruments their doctors used, what their brothels looked like, what their election notices or for-rent signs were like—the list could be extended endlessly.

Pompeii was founded as an agricultural village perhaps as early as the eighth century B.C. It grew into a town when, in the late fifth century B.C., it was taken over by the aggressive Italic people called the Samnites. These built the first true houses there, one-story buildings that turned inward, like the traditional homes in Spanish America. To the street they presented almost blank walls. Windowless, or near windowless, rooms surrounded an atrium hall in the front of the house, and the rear enclosed a patio or garden. The atrium had a roof that sloped inward to a large square opening so that rain could fall from it into a pool below and into a cistern underneath that.

The community throve. It was flanked by fields of rich volcanic soil, and it stood on the shore of the Bay of Naples; it was in a position to profit agriculturally and commercially. Early in the first century B.C. Rome moved in, took over political control, and brought the town into the embrace of its widening domains. Roman families then joined, in many cases no doubt drove out, the Samnite families, and the building of new homes went on apace. These retained the general design of the old-fashioned houses, the atrium and patio, but introduced numerous variations to increase grace and comfort: an enlarged patio with bedrooms opening off it, a cloistered garden behind, duplicate salons for winter and summer use respectively, and so on. The establishment of the Roman Empire under Augustus brought the same prosperity to Pompeii that it had elsewhere; there grew up a substantial trade in agricultural products, particularly wine, and in textiles. The middle class, just as at Rome, grew bigger and richer. Now they too could afford homes as substantial as those of the local gentry, but by this time the provincial little town was running out of space. And so we find some of the very wealthy moving to the suburbs, where they erected elegant villas set in open ground and commanding lovely views of the sea and mountains; the famous Villa of the Mysteries, so called because its walls are decorated with scenes of an initiation into some mystic religious cult, was one of these. It was still possible for a rich man to build himself an elaborate mansion in town—the sumptuous House of the Vettii, which every guided tour to Pompeii includes, was put up by a pair of successful merchants no more than two decades before the fatal eruption. But such houses were becoming increasingly rare. More commonly the old-fashioned stately homes were taken over for the town's commercial needs. One of Pompeii's specialties was the processing of textiles and cleaning of garments; the establishments were all installed in remodeled private houses, with troughs for steeping cloth sitting amid the elegance of columned porticoes. One fine, venerable residence, the so-called House of Sallust, was partly made over into business property, with a second floor clapped on it to accommodate additional rooms and its façade altered to allow for a street-front bar; it reminds one of the *palazzi* in Florence or Rome that now accommodate shops, offices, or tourist *pensioni*. Along the main streets the practice of putting up buildings with two floors was growing. At the moment of its death Pompeii was still a provincial town, its population some twenty-five thousand at the most, in which families had each their own home; had it lived on and continued to grow at the same rate, almost certainly wholesale demolition would have started to make way for blocks of flats, as at Rome and Ostia.

Pompeii's houses line the streets with no open space between, in front, or in back. This is because, as mentioned earlier, they embrace their own open space: a house of any pretension included at the rear its patio, a miniature cloister surrounded by the family bedrooms. What is most striking about all the homes, whether mansions or modest dwellings, is the richness of the interior decoration. Pompeians with money obviously liked to spend it on feathering their nests: they covered their walls with murals, often including copies by local artists of famed Greek paintings; they paved the floors with mosaics; they filled niches, porticoes, angles, and other suitable spots with stone or bronze statuary, again mostly copies of Greek masterpieces. Portrait busts of the greats of the past—Demosthenes, Epicurus, and the like—were also a favored

Street in Pompeii. The surface is carefully paved and is spanned at intervals by large steppingstones to enable pedestrians to cross without dirtying their feet. The large openings on the left are the front entrances of shops.

form of décor, and it was common to set up in the atrium one of the master of the house himself. These are fascinating: faithfully reproducing the subject, they show us in unvarnished fashion what the good burghers who could afford these homes looked like.

Pompeii's public buildings are much the same as those found in all provincial Roman towns—much the same, aside from size and grandeur, as those in Rome itself. There were three bath complexes located to serve three different areas of the city. The entertainment facilities were on the edge of town, an amphitheatre accommodating some twenty thousand for gladiatorial combats and two theatres for musical and stage events, one open and large seating about five thousand, the other covered and small seating about one thousand. The government buildings were all clustered about the forum: city hall, meeting place of the town council, law court, and two important temples, to Jupiter and Apollo. Also flanking the forum was an elaborate food market, an enclosed square with small shops for selling various items along one side, a large room in one corner for selling fish and meat, and a pen with live animals for customers seeking sacrificial victims. Alongside the forum, too, was the headquarters of one of those clubs that played so important a role in Roman urban life, in this instance the society of fullers, that is, processors of new cloth and cleaners of garments, perhaps the most prestigious trade association of the town. It was a sumptuous building with an ample open court surrounded by a corridor and garnished with a two-level colonnade. The fullers owed it to the generosity of a certain Eumachia, a lady who was not only charitable but good-looking, as we can tell from the statue the grateful society set up in her honor in a prominently placed recess.

Pompeii's officialdom consisted of two duumvirs, mayors with added judicial authority; two aediles, or commissioners of streets, markets, baths, and entertainment; and a town council of one hundred selected substantial citizens. The government was remarkably efficient. Streets were paved in the same solid fashion as Rome's great highways, had sidewalks, and even had steppingstones so that pedestrians could cross without messing their sandaled feet with the mud and dung in the road. At various key points were watering troughs for animals. And the amphitheatre and theatres, together with the numerous notices that have been found announcing lavish gladiatorial combats, make it clear that the aediles gave due attention to public entertainment.

The Pompeians had their fair share of the age-old means for entertaining themselves—bars, taverns, restaurants, and brothels. The thirsty had no trouble locating the nearest bar or tavern: these were instantly identifiable by the characteristic counter opening onto the street to serve customers who wanted just a quick glass of wine. The taverns included rooms behind for more leisurely drinking or for eating, and chambers on a floor above for any who wanted to satisfy the sexual appetite as well. The décor was usually referential, wall paintings showing the locale in action, guests eating, drinking, gaming, quarreling. Sometimes these are embellished with captions. A painting of a waiter pouring out wine for a customer is accompanied by the written instruction, "Add cold water—but just a wee bit!" In another we see two customers seated at a table placing dice. One has just thrown and announces triumphantly, "I'm out!" The other replies, "No! It's three 2's." There follows a second scene in which we see three figures, all on their feet. The first two are our pair of gamblers, and one is saying, "So strike me dead—I swear I won!" The second calls him a filthy obscenity and shouts, "*I* won!" And the third, the proprietor, pushing the two toward the door, says, "Go on outside to do your fighting!"

Pompeii had at least twenty-five brothels, including one that was designed to handle multiple clients: it had ten chambers—tiny dark cells—on two levels, each decorated formally with a painting showing a version of the sex act, and informally with the clients' scribbled comments.

As a matter of fact, it is the handwriting on the walls that, more than anything else, brings Pompeii alive to us. We can sense what politics was like from the many election notices preserved: in Pompeii these were written on the outside walls of houses and shops, some in the rough printing of a casual supporter, others in the handsome lettering of a hired professional. They run to formulas, as ours tend to do: "Make Marcus Marius aedile. A good man!"; "The goldsmiths unanimously endorse the election of Gaius Cuspius Pansa as aedile"; "Satia and Petronia ask you to elect Marcus Casellius and Lucius Albucius. May we always have such citizens in our community!"; "Genialis urges the election of Bruttius Balbus as duumvir. He will be the watch-dog of our treasury!" (not too free a translation of *hic aerarium conservabit,* "he will preserve the treasury"). One candidate for aedile campaigned so hard (there are more than a dozen notices supporting his election) that he caught the attention of Pompeii's jokesters: among the groups that declare their adherence are the *Dormientes universi,* "the Sleepyheads en masse," the *Seri Bibi universi,* "the Drunken Stay-Out-Lates en masse," the sneak thieves, and a chap who signs himself *Verus Innocens,* "Mr. I. B. Honest."

In the absence of television, newspapers, magazines, and other such modern media, the Pompeians used their walls for all sorts of public notices. We find announcements of gladiatorial shows ("The troupe of gladiators of the aedile, Aulus Suettius Certus, will be fighting at Pompeii May 31. Also a wild-beast hunt. Awnings will be provided"—no small inducement for an audience required to spend a whole day under the Mediterranean sun in early summer), of property for rent ("In the Arrius Pollio block, Gnaeus Alleius Nigidius Maius prop., to let from the 1st of next July, shops with living quarters, high-class second-story apartments, a house. Interested parties please apply to Primus, slave of Gnaeus Alleius Nigidius Maius"), of lost objects ("A copper pot has been taken from this shop. 65 sesterces [about $260] reward for whoever brings it back, 20 sesterces [about $8.00] for identifying the thief so we can get our property back"). Then there are the graffiti pure and simple, random scribblings of every possible kind, from records of winning bets to the number of steps it took one houseowner to walk the length of his patio. Someone named Paris wrote *Paris hic fuit* nineteen hundred years before the world ever heard of Kilroy. *Staphilus hic cum Quieta,* "Staphylus was here with Quieta," on a house wall is more or less the Pompeian equivalent of our "John loves Mary" on a tree trunk. (Staphylus had a way with girls; another graffito reads *Romula hic cum Staphylo moratur,* "Romula dallies here with Staphylus"). Pompeians defaced walls with exactly the same kind of obscenities found in public toilets today. They even scribbled inside their houses: children practiced their ABC's on the walls of their rooms, and a mural in a home that the excavator sentimentally ascribes to a pair of newlyweds has scratched on it, "Lovers, like bees, lead a honeyed life." As a matter of fact, graffiti were so ubiquitous that people wrote graffiti about them: in three different public places we find the jingle: "I marvel you don't collapse, O walls, / beneath the burden of so many scrawls."

Pompeii illustrates one aspect of Roman life. Another is revealed by Ostia, the city that served as the port of Rome. Its ruins lie at the mouth of the Tiber River, some fifteen miles downstream from the capital. Pompeii, with its provincial air, one-family homes, houses that were leftovers from a more leisurely lifestyle, bygone elegance still abundantly visible, reminds one of some of our New England towns that have passed their prime. Ostia is an ancient Weehawken or Jersey City, a city of docks and warehouses and offices, of businessmen who dealt not in oxcarts of wine for nearby neighbors but in cargoes of it, and of grain and olive oil and all the other imports, down to lions for the Colosseum, that Rome needed; a city of work gangs who manned the yards, wharves, barges, ferries, lofts.

Ostia's history matches that of our Fort Dodge or Santa Fe: it began, in the fourth century B.C., as the site of a fort, to keep enemies from penetrating the river. Within a century or so it started to assume the role it was to play for the next six to seven hundred years, the point where cargoes for Rome were unloaded, stored, and forwarded upriver. As Rome grew, so did Ostia, becoming by Augustus's time a flourishing entrepôt, despite the fact that the mouth of the river, exposed to wind and weather, made a poor harbor. In the second half of the first century A.D. this was rectified: Claudius started, Nero completed, and Trajan expanded a magnificent manmade port some two miles to the north. It brought more business than ever to Ostia, and the town entered upon its halcyon days, when it supported a population of perhaps fifty thousand. This was exactly during the period that particularly interests us, the second century A.D.: the streets upon streets of houses, shops, and public buildings whose ruins we walk through today were for the most part put up during the reigns of Trajan, Hadrian, and Antoninus Pius.

In the very heart of Ostia the walls of the old fort still stand, buried amid the structures raised around them when the town burst their bonds, as commerce rather than defense became the focus of existence. In the quarters nearby are remains here and there of spacious private houses with atrium and patio, like those in Pompeii, relics of a time when there still was land to spare. But as the population swelled, Ostia, just like today's burgeoning commercial centers, was forced to build vertically. It became a small-scale Rome, a city of apartment houses. They stood one alongside the other, all three or four stories high, usually with shops occupying the part of the ground floor that opened on the street. They were built of concrete faced with brick, and though doorways were tricked out with pilasters or engaged columns and similar architectural decoration, and the second floors adorned with balconies, Ostia's streets must have presented the same monotonous appearance as their counterparts in our cities.

The town housed all classes of people, from the slaves who sweated on the docks to the bankers who financed the cargoes. For the poor there were tenements with cramped quarters in the older parts of town. For the middle and upper classes there was housing of all grades, the finest being in blocks of handsome garden apartments, each complex standing alone in an open area. The flats in them, presumably among the best Ostia offered, show that even well-to-do families made do with minimal space. The buildings were oblong, and each floor was quartered into four identical oblong five-room apartments. These extended from the middle of the building to the corners: at the inner end were a main and service entrance and the kitchen; from here ran a wide corridor that, passing three interior chambers lighted only indirectly from the corridor windows, ended at a fine large room with double exposure at the corner of the building. This last must have served as both dining and living room, and the windowless chambers as bedrooms. There were no bathrooms; the families surely used commodes, and then there were the latrines in a set of public baths just a short distance away. Excavators have so far unearthed sixteen such bath complexes; every quarter of the town had one conveniently nearby.

Who lived in these elegant apartments? We get some clues from the names in the many inscriptions and tomb plaques that have been uncovered. They reveal that the population of Ostia, like its streets, was a replica in miniature of Rome. There was an upper crust of established Roman and Italian gentry who monopolized the honorary and political offices of the town. Below them was a large well-to-do middle class that ran the port's trades and supplied its services. Its members were for the most part of foreign origin, people from all over the Mediterranean, from France and Spain and North Africa as well as Greece and the Near

East, who had arrived as slaves and earned their freedom. And below them was the horde of slaves who did the blue-collar work.

The ruins of Ostia include well-preserved examples of commercial buildings—warehouses, lofts, offices. One of the most remarkable complexes is a spacious forumlike area behind the theatre that modern archaeologists have dubbed the Piazzale delle Corporazioni, "Corporation Square." Three sides of a vast square are surrounded by a colonnade, and opening on it is a line of small offices. The colonnade has a mosaic paving, and in front of many of the offices this includes an identifying picture and inscription: "The Shippers of Narbo (Narbonne)," with a picture of a freighter passing the lighthouse of the harbor; "The Shippers of Carthage," with a picture of two freighters passing the lighthouse, and so on. Anyone searching for a passage to, say, Carthage did not have to tramp the waterfront endlessly questioning but simply went to the office here and found out when the next ship was expected to leave.

The ruins include, as we would expect, examples of club headquarters. An inscription found in place identifies that of the Builders' Association, a handsome two-story structure whose ground floor encompassed an open court and portico, at least five dining rooms, chapel, kitchen, and latrine. The upper floor probably had committee rooms and bedrooms.

When, in A.D. 331, Constantine shifted the capital of the empire to his new foundation of Constantinople, Rome began to go rapidly downhill. Inevitably it dragged Ostia down with it—fewer and fewer freighters put into the harbor, and the town was left with less and less to keep it alive. What activity there was the port, now the nucleus of a good-sized community, handled by itself. People drifted away, and downtown Ostia soon began to show typical signs of urban blight—houses either totally derelict or with the upper floors walled up and just the lower occupied. There was one brief period of revival, when, in the fourth century A.D., the town became a popular summer resort for the very wealthy; excavation has uncovered the remains of the sumptuous villas they built for themselves in the quarters nearest the shore. But this soon flickered out. The remaining population departed for better prospects elsewhere, and malaria, flourishing in the now-neglected marshy land all about, killed off the few who tried to stay on. The harbor, no longer attended, silted up; today some of the structures of Rome's international airport stand where Roman freighters used to moor.

Unlike Pompeii, Ostia died a slow and lingering death. For centuries it lay abandoned, a graveyard of ruins. Builders cannibalized its crumbling stones, treasure hunters carried off its fallen sculptures. Not until 1909 did systematic excavation begin. Since then, however, Italian archaeologists have resurrected at least half of the ancient city and patched and restored the ruins with such care that today one can spend hours walking its streets and prowling about its buildings. Pompeii offers charm, variety, and fascinating glimpses of its bustling, occasionally gracious, small-town way of life. Ostia offers an unvarnished look at a hard-working commercial town—such as Rome itself was, once one walked away from the grandeur of its public monuments.

CHAPTER VIII

The Soldier

Sometime in the second century A.D. a young fellow named Apion left his little village in Egypt to join the navy. He was promptly shipped to the great base at Misenum near Naples, and from there he wrote his first letter home: "Dear Father,

"First of all, I hope you are well and will always be well, and my sister and her daughter and my brother. I thank the God Serapis that when I was in danger on the sea he quickly came to the rescue. When I arrived at Misenum I received from the government three gold pieces for my traveling expenses. I'm fine. Please write me, Father, first to tell me that you are well, second that my sister and brother are well, and third so that I can kiss your hand because you gave me a good education and because of it I hope to get quick promotion if the gods are willing. Love to Capiton and my brother and sister and Serenilla and my friends. I've given Euctemon a picture of myself to bring to you. My name is now Antonius Maximus, my ship the *Athenonice*. Goodbye.

"P.S. Serenus, Agathodaemon's son, sends regards, and so does Turbo, Gallonius' son."

The address indicates that he sent it with a serviceman or courier who was headed for an army camp in Egypt (the invention of a public post lay a millennium and a half in the future), whence it was duly delivered by someone passing by where his father lived. It was read, discarded in the course of time, and lay in Egypt's perennially dry sands undisturbed until the last century, when diggers unearthed it.

Apion was lucky: he had met some other boys from his home town, had been assigned duty with the main naval arm, and, thanks to his education, saw bright chances of getting ahead. Like any recruit in any age, he hungers for news from home and sends the family a picture of himself, a miniature (the camera lay even further ahead than the postal service), very likely in his new uniform. And now that he is in the Roman navy, he drops his Egyptian name for a good Roman one.

In every province of the empire there were young fellows just as eager as Apion to join the armed forces, even though it meant not a stint of merely a few years, as today, but a lifetime: a hitch in the army was twenty to twenty-five years, in the navy twenty-six. No matter—they offered a respected profession, modest but decent pay, good opportunities for promotion, and at the end, citizenship for the noncitizen. For men on the lower rungs of the social ladder, this was plenty.

The soldiers in the armies of the republic, even the vast aggregations that Caesar or Antony or Brutus and Cassius had led, had all been irregulars: they signed on for a campaign or series of campaigns and at the end were paid off. It was Augustus who founded a standing army and navy.

The imperial army was surprisingly small, some three hundred thousand men to guard a domain that stretched from Scotland to Syria. Half the force consisted of the legions, those famed units that carried eagles as their standards, bore distinctive names and numbers, and were recruited only from among the citizen body. There were twenty-eight to thirty of these divisions, as we would call them, with an average strength of fifty-five hundred men. Backing up the legions were the auxiliaries or colonial troops, recruited from the various peoples in the empire. At the outset they fought in their native fashion with their native weapons, but as time went on, they were more and more assimilated to the legions' way of fighting. On discharge they were granted citizenship. For a lucky few there was service in the Praetorian Guard, the legion stationed in Rome at the emperor's side. The navy, which young Apion joined, was very much the junior service in the armed forces. As in the auxiliaries, its men were provincials and were rewarded with citizenship on discharge.

The Praetorian Guard not only made the most money but enjoyed living amid the pleasures that the capital afforded. Even the sailors were not so badly off in this respect: the main naval base was on the Bay of Naples, and the next in importance at Ravenna. But the men of the legions and auxiliary troops were stationed far from the fleshpots of Rome or other urban centers, in a wide arc on or near the frontiers of the empire: in the second century A.D. there were three legions in Britain, one in Spain, four along the Rhine and eleven along the Danube, nine in the Near East, one in North Africa. Since large-scale wars were few, the men tended to be left where they were: not a few joined, served, and lived out their days in and around the local army base.

When a boy, usually in his early twenties, decided to join the armed forces, he reported to the nearest recruiting station with his documents—this was to prove whether he was a citizen and eligible for the legions or a provincial and eligible only for the auxiliaries or the navy. He had his height checked (the minimum for the army was five feet eight inches) and took a physical examination. If accepted, he was given 75 denarii (some $1,200, which, though called travel money, was actually a bounty for joining), was administered the oath, and was then packed off to boot camp for basic training. He ran and jumped to harden his physique, learned to swim, practiced marching with the standard military pace, which enabled troops to cover fifteen miles in five hours, and took lessons in handling the legionary's standard weapon, the short sword; at the outset he hacked with a wooden sword at a wooden stake, a technique introduced into the army from the gladiator schools. When once in condition, he was made to march with full pack, sixty pounds of weapons, tools, and rations. He was then ready for training in the various movements, to form at command a single line, double line, wedge, circle, square, and the *testudo,* "tortoise,"

Roman Soldier. A legionary with standard equipment of helmet, short sword, and shield. Early second century A.D. Detail from Trajan's Column, Rome.

the special square for storming city walls, in which the men covered
themselves with a carapace of shields. He was taught, too, how to do his
part in pitching camp, a protective procedure that Roman armies on
the march took every night; it involved digging a ditch all about the
camping area and raising behind it a mound surmounted by a palisade
of stakes.

Though the emphasis was naturally on combat, most of the men, as
it turned out, needed their weapons only for maneuvers, inasmuch as
the first two centuries of the Roman Empire were, apart from a few
bloody but short wars, years of peace. But if Roman soldiers were
spared risk, they paid for it in hard labor on public works. It was they
who erected and maintained many of the empire's bridges and aqueducts, who dug its canals and cisterns, who above all were responsible
for most of its great network of roads: intended first and foremost for
military use, these were laid out by army surveyors and engineers and
built by army muscle. "I thank Serapis and Lady Luck," writes a young
soldier in A.D. 107 from Bostra in the desert tract south of Damascus to
his mother in Egypt, "while everybody is slaving all day long cutting
stones, since I'm a noncom, I go around doing nothing." The writer
obviously knew the ropes: in another letter, to his father, he makes the
same boast and explains that he managed to get himself appointed
librarius legionis, one of the divisional clerks, which ensured his wielding
a stylus instead of a sledge.

The first step on the ladder of promotion was into such specialties as
clerk, armorer, orderly, trumpeter, and so on; they brought a man no
extra pay, but they spared him much fatigue duty. From here he could
move up into the noncommissioned ranks: *signifer,* "standard bearer";
optio, or sergeant; *tesserarius,* or master sergeant; *cornicularius,* or sergeant
major. The step after that was the big one, to centurion, or lieutenant.
There were no officer-training schools in the Roman army; promotion
to centurion, the lowest commissioned rank, was generally from below.
The man who made it then worked to rise higher, since each legion had
various grades of centurion corresponding roughly to our ranks from
lieutenant to major. Officers above the rank of centurion were neces-

sarily commissioned from outside, for they were drawn exclusively from the two highest levels of Roman society; the *legatus legionis,* commanding officer of a legion, corresponding to a general in charge of a division, had to come from the upper senatorial class, his next in command from the lower, the others from the gentry just under the senatorial class.

Augustus set the legionary's pay at 225 denarii a year (some $3,600), and even this very modest amount was lessened by deductions for the cost of weapons, clothing, and rations. By the second century A.D. the figure had been raised to 300 denarii. Noncoms got pay and a half, senior noncoms double pay. In addition there were windfalls: an emperor often included in his will special bonuses to be paid on his death (Augustus and Tiberius each willed every legionary a third of a year's pay) or issued them on accession. There was also generous separation pay for the legions; during Augustus's time it was 3,000 denarii or just about thirteen years' pay. The auxiliaries and the navy received less than half of what the legions got and no separation pay; perhaps the citizenship they were granted was considered an adequate equivalent.

The one branch of the service whose wages were far out of line was the Praetorian Guard. The emperors had to have the support of these men, strategically located right in Rome, and from as early as the reign of Tiberius, their method was to buy it. The regular wage, to begin with, was three times that of the legionaries. On top of this, each emperor on accession literally poured money into their laps to ensure their allegiance: Claudius gave them 3,750 denarii (some $60,000), Nero the same, Marcus Aurelius 5,000. The nadir came in A.D. 193, when the Praetorians murdered the ruling emperor, announced they would hand over the throne to whoever offered the biggest bonus, and held a veritable auction with two aspirants bidding against each other. The guards had become kingmakers instead of soldiers, and the formidable Septimius Severus, after toppling the successful bidder later in the year, took the inevitable step of abolishing them. He replaced them with a new guard recruited from the legions he most trusted.

A Roman soldier's return to civilian life upon discharge normally involved no such jolts as it does today. As mentioned before, the men tended to join units stationed in their vicinity and to spend their time in service there. They were not allowed to marry, since the state wanted them to be free of family responsibilities; yet, since it also wanted a continuing supply of manpower for the armed forces, it encouraged them to form liaisons with local women and twisted the law to give quasi-legitimacy to their offspring. Thus many a veteran simply continued to live on where he had been based, where he had founded a family. Often he had the pleasure of seeing a son replace him in the ranks and, profiting from having a father who was an ex-serviceman and could pull strings, move up faster and higher than he had. Veterans often retired with the money and respect to make them pillars of society in the modest communities where they settled down—like Lucius Caecilius Optatus, centurion of the legion VII Gemina Felix in Spain, who, an inscription found at Barcino (Barcelona today) tells us, had

been honorably discharged by the Emperors Marcus Aurelius Antoninus and Lucius Aurelius Verus, been selected by the town of Barcino to be among those exempted from public charges, and achieved the office of aedile and three times the office of duumvir. . . . He left a legacy to the municipality of Barcino as follows: I . . . bequeath . . . 7,500 denarii [about $120,000], with the six per cent interest on which I desire a boxing contest to be held each year on June 10 at a cost of up to 250 denarii and on the same day 200 denarii of oil to be supplied to the public in the public baths.

CHAPTER IX

Many Gods

The remains of the temples of Saturn, Concord, Vesta, Castor and Pollux, and of various deified emperors, ring the forum. Above, on the Capitoline Hill, stood the temple of the mighty Jupiter Optimus Maximus. Caesar's forum held the temple of Venus Genetrix, Augustus's of Mars Ultor, Nerva's of Minerva—the list could go on and on. During the long centuries of the empire, these houses for the worship of Rome's various gods were never neglected; on the deity's festival days they were without fail the scene of ceremony, sacrifice, and prayer. Yet, as time passed, less and less religious spirit infused what went on in them. They were maintained not so much for the gods' sake as for the state's, to stand as a manifest symbol of Romanism and provide a focal point for a feeling of belonging among the vastly diverse people of the empire: to serve, in effect, the cause of patriotism rather than religion. This was patently the case with the well-organized emperor cult, the worship of the spirits of Caesar, Augustus, Tiberius, Claudius, and others who, by decree of the subservient Senate, had been deified upon their death. "Oh, dear," the earthy Vespasian is reported to have said when he was on the point of dying, "I think I'm becoming a god."

Traditional Roman religion by no means disappeared. Outside urban areas it was as strong as ever; not for nothing did the word "pagan," which literally means "countryman," come to be applied to its adherents. Peasants continued to sacrifice to the ancient gods of the fields and flocks as they had always done, continued to carry out punctiliously the rituals they had learned from their fathers. Even the sophisticated urbanite stood by old customs: until late Roman times houses still had a shrine or niche for the lar, the god of the household, and people still left lighted lamps or offerings there—although most often it surely was a mechanical act, the result of habit and not conviction. Some gods actually gained ground. The cult of Hercules throve: a heroic figure who selflessly devoted his mighty strength to freeing mankind from assorted evils had an understandable appeal.

There was yet another way in which the old gods lived on, through the ease with which Rome practiced syncretism, the melding of deities of similar characteristics but different origins. The Romans had early absorbed the Greek gods this way, assimilating Zeus to Jupiter, Hermes to Mercury, Athena to Minerva, and so on. Now they did the same to gods of all nations whose lands were overrun in the expansion of the empire. Roman soldiers in Celtic Britain, impressed by the power of a local war god, worshiped Mars Belatucader; soldiers and sailors all over the empire offered sacrifice and prayer to Jupiter Dolichenus, a union of Jupiter and a god from the inner reaches of Asia Minor whose origins may go back to Hittite times. One reason for the difficulties experienced first by Jews and then by Christians was the lofty exclusiveness of their supreme deity; such behavior was unparalleled among the multitude of other foreign divinities the Romans encountered.

But the traditional gods, even when invigorated by syncretistic unions, found it hard to meet the challenge of certain deities who, for three centuries before Augustus founded the empire, had been moving steadily westward from their homes in the east.

Zeus, Apollo, Athena, and the other members of the Greek pantheon had arisen to serve not individuals but city-states, the small homogeneous political units that were so characteristically Greek. When

Alexander and his successors brought these under their rule and made them part of large-scale monarchies, their citizens quickly felt the need for some more personal form of worship. In the regions through which he had led his armies were religions that offered just this, religions that inspired a votary to forget his daily life in an intense emotional experience, or to look beyond it in the expectation of an ultimate salvation. They had all along affected a limited number of Greeks who had come in contact with them; on the heels of Alexander's conquests they moved out of their homelands in Asia Minor, Syria, and Egypt to gain converts throughout the Greek-speaking east. By the first century B.C. they were seeping steadily westward. The Roman Empire, with its network of roads, trade routes, and sea lanes, its unceasing shuttling back and forth of merchants, officials, and soldiers, made their path easy. Isis, Serapis, Cybele, Babylonian astrologers—all soon were conquering new lands as far away as the shores of the Atlantic.

Egypt gave the Roman Empire the worship of Serapis and Isis—above all, Isis, the goddess whose unswerving dedication to her husband, Osiris, succeeded in raising him from the dead after his evil brother killed him, whose devoted attention to her child, Horus, succeeded in making of him her husband's avenger. As the ideal wife and mother, her appeal was to both men and women, but particularly women, who had few friends in the traditional Greek or Roman pantheon; a virgin huntress or a girl who had never had a mother and went around in man's armor hardly suited their needs. "I am Isis," runs the hymn her congregations sang, "I am she whom women call goddess. . . . I brought wife and husband together. I ruled that women should bear offspring after nine months. I ordained that children should love their parents. . . . I compelled men to love women. . . . I invented the marriage contract."

In her worship there were priestesses as well as priests. The syncretism of the age melded her with Demeter, Aphrodite, Artemis, and other Mediterranean goddesses; she absorbed every one of them—she was the all-powerful queen of heaven, earth, and the underworld, giver of health, beauty, love, abundance, wisdom.

Isis had her difficulties in gaining a foothold in the city of Rome. After sweeping over Greece and the Greek isles and making her way through Sicily and southern Italy, she arrived there in the early decades of the first century B.C. But the hard-nosed rulers of the late republic were suspicious of Egypt politically and morally: they looked upon Isis's shrines as centers of subversion laced with licentiousness. Time and again decrees were passed banning her worship, but it always returned. Under the empire such attempts were finally dropped and, indeed, from Caligula on, Rome's rulers along with their subjects embraced her cult. There was a grandiose shrine of Isis right in the Campus Martius not far from the Pantheon; no trace of it has survived, but many of the statues and monuments that once decorated it have. Four of the obelisks that now stand in various parts of Rome come from it—the one in front of the Pantheon, the one atop Bernini's fountain in the Piazza Navona, another not far from the railroad station, and the little one that rides the back of a stone elephant near the rear of the Pantheon.

Her priests, dressed in linen robes—they were forbidden to wear wool—and with shaven heads, conducted services twice a day, chanting prayers to the sound of the sistrum, the special rattle required by her worship; holy water was sprinkled about, preferably water from Isis's own river, the Nile. The first service was held in the dim light of early dawn; the priest began it by drawing back the curtain of the inner sanctuary and revealing to the congregation their deity's holy image, a young matron holding in her arms the infant Horus. The second service came in the afternoon. And twice a year there were great festivals in her honor: in November to celebrate the resurrection of her husband, and in March, the opening of the sailing season—for Isis among all her other attributes was patron goddess of mariners. The ceremony in March included a joyous and colorful procession in which her adherents, dressed in fantastic costumes, accompanied her sacred boat to the shore and launched it; some see in the occasion the origins of our carnival. Isis's priests were a professional clergy, devoted to her service for a lifetime; they took a vow of chastity and were hemmed about by taboos—in addition to the ban on wool garments, they were forbidden to drink wine or to eat pork or fish or certain vegetables. Her initiates were equally dedicated. They waited for her "call," some of them for years; when it came, and when they had finally gone through the mystic and solemn initiation, they emerged into a blaze of light, torches in hand, and were exhibited to the congregation as gods themselves, their souls forever freed from fate and death.

Isis most frequently was worshiped along with Serapis, a conflation of Zeus and an Egyptian deity deliberately created either by Alexander or by Ptolemy I, who took over Egypt at his death. Serapis's synthetic origin appparently had scant effect on his appeal. He too offered salvation, and in addition he had the gift of healing the sick. The seat of his worship was the vast Serapeum in Alexandria, where his great cult-statue with golden head and jeweled eyes gleamed in its darkened shrine. When Christians sacked the place in A.D. 391, it was a sign to the world that their religion had finally triumphed.

Isis and Serapis provided soothing and abiding spiritual comfort and the reassurance that comes from daily services conducted by a responsible clergy. Other Eastern religions offered headier stuff, emotional catharsis, moments of pure ecstasy in which the votary totally blotted out reality and lost himself in the act of adoration. Cybele, the Great Mother goddess, had come to Rome from Phrygia in Asia Minor as early as 204 B.C., when she was taken there to lend her powerful aid in defeating Hannibal. She never left. Moreover, as time went on, in the syncretistic manner of the age, she took over practices and rituals that belonged to other goddesses of the Near East, such as Phoenicia's Astarte and Syria's Atargatis. According to the legend, she was in love with the glorious youth Attis, who, like Isis's Osiris, died and was resurrected. But in Attis's story there was an element of wild passion—Cybele grieved in frenzy at his loss, greeted his rebirth with equally frenzied delight, and castrated him when, after she had become worn and plain, he spurned her. Her ceremony was awesomely impressive and at the same time wildly barbaric. The goddess was carried about in a monumental chariot, and her devotees danced to the pounding of tom-toms, clashing of cymbals, and shrilling of pipes. During the rites that commemorated her grief, her priests, all native Phrygians, light-headed from a week of fasting and keyed up for the occasion, lacerated themselves with knives until arms and shoulders flowed with blood. The excitement rose to a crescendo, and at its climax some novices were so transported as to carry out upon themselves the irrevocable act that gained them entry to the priesthood and forever joined them with the goddess—castration.

Cybele's worship became so widespread that its excesses had to be toned down to conform to the tastes of its steadily expanding circle of adherents. By the middle of the first century A.D. offices in her hier-archy were being filled by men and women of respectable families. The priests no longer had to be eunuchs, and this opened the ranks to local burghers. But many still were; Saint Augustine saw them, with po-maded hair and make-up, begging in the streets of Carthage. In the second century A.D. her followers added to her rites the *taurobolium,* or baptism in blood, a messy practice much favored in certain Asian cults: the votary stood in a pit closed over by a grating, and as a bull was sacrificed upon it, he bathed himself in the blood that rained down, thereby becoming, as inscriptions commemorating the occasion pro-claim, *in aeternum renatus,* "renewed forever." Since the slaughter of no inexpensive victim was required, it must have been the wealthier mem-bers of her flock who went in for such renewal.

Not all the salvation cults came from the Near East. Many of the so-called mystery religions, whose members were initiated in a secret ceremony and then worshiped with a secret ritual they were sworn never to divulge, arose on Greek soil. The famous Eleusinian mysteries of Demeter and Persephone, goddesses of the crops, were celebrated at Eleusis, some twelve miles from Athens. There were any number of others, but the ones that most affected the Roman world were the Dionysiac mysteries. Dionysus was the god both of wine and of the emotional release that comes from it. His women devotees were called maenads, a word that derives from a root meaning "to be mad," and in the numerous sculptures and paintings we have of them, they are always depicted in the act of dancing with mad abandon, seeking to be freed from themselves, to be totally possessed by the god and thereby forever assured of his divine protection. Numerous stone coffins have been found with scenes of the legend of Dionysus carved on them: Dionysus discovering his future bride Ariadne asleep on the island of Naxos where the faithless Theseus had deserted her, Dionysus with Ariadne at his side returning from a triumphal campaign in distant lands. Presumably those laid to rest in the coffins were devotees looking forward to a like union and sharing of triumphs with the god. Exactly what went on in his ceremonies we do not know; his initiates have respected their vow of silence. A clue may lie in the paintings on the walls of the so-called Villa of the Mysteries in Pompeii. Here we see a young girl undergoing an initiation ceremony that involves, among other steps, a frightening flagellation. She may have been dedicating herself to Dionysus or perhaps to the deity of some other mystery cult; in any event, the result anticipated was the same, to make her one of the chosen and enable her to count on the god's eternal favor.

Toward the end of the second century A.D. a religion came to the fore that, in its austerity and stern moral demands, stands in sharp contrast with the others of the age—the worship of Mithras. Its homeland was Persia. Persian religion conceived of two divine powers forever in opposition, Ahura-Mazda, lord of life and light, and Ahriman, lord of death and darkness. Mithras was the intermediary between mankind and Ahura-Mazda: the lord of light created him, so the legend went, from a rock and made him his attendant and agent, allied with the Sun, in the everlasting struggle against the lord of darkness. Of the many labors he carried out in this cause the one his Roman worshipers chose to emphasize was his struggle with the first living creature, the bull. He overcame it and dragged it to a cave; it escaped, and the Sun dispatched a raven as messenger to inform him that his duty was to find and slay the creature. This he did, and from the bull's blood flowed all the plenty of nature. Then the first human couple was born, and Mithras strove successfully to overcome the plague and flame that Ahriman sent to destroy them. His labors were then over, and after a final feast he was

Mithraic Chapel. Worshipers reclined with feet to the wall and heads toward
the ledge on which was placed the ritual meal. A relief showing Mithras slay-
ing a bull decorates the altar. Third century A.D. Beneath the Church of San
Clemente, Rome.

carried in the chariot of the Sun to heaven, where he watches over the
welfare of the faithful.

There were seven grades of initiates in the worship of Mithras.
A votary started with the rank of Raven and rose through the ranks
of Hidden One, Soldier, Lion, Persian, and Sun-Runner to Father,
who presided over the ceremonies. These were held in small, narrow
chapels—either underground or shut off from the light in order to give
the effect of Mithras's cave—which were decorated with sacred scenes,
especially of Mithras killing the bull. Here the members gathered
dressed in the costume of their rank, and in the course of the rites, they
cawed, growled, and made other appropriate sounds. There was no

professional clergy; what direction was needed was supplied by the Father. The congregations were small, for when the number increased beyond what was considered desirable, a new group formed and built its own chapel. This is why we find so many of them: there are forty-five known chapels of Mithras in Rome; and Ostia, whose population from late in the second century A.D. on could not have been over fifty thousand, had at least fifteen.

Mithras was a god of lofty goals, the ever-victorious protector of mankind, and his worship, despite the element of abracadabra in its ritual, made stern demands on its devotees: they were to be not only resolute and courageous but morally pure, like the god they served; some in their enthusiasm practiced a degree of asceticism. It was solely a man's religion, however; there was no place in it for women. Soldiers in particular responded to the appeal of a god whose assignment, like theirs, was to protect people and who had never been conquered. The Roman army was in good part responsible for his rapid spread from the east over the whole of the empire; his distinctive windowless chapels have been found as far away as London. With its emotional appeal and its strong moral dimension, Mithraism throughout the third century A.D. was Christianity's most serious rival in the struggle for people's hearts.

Is there a clear line dividing the maenad in ecstasy, the frenzied priest who lacerates himself, the initiate cawing like a raven, from the Roman racetrack fanatic who calls demons down on a team he wishes to lose? Where does religion end and superstition begin? If there is such a line, it was not easy to draw during the days of the Roman Empire. To millions of its people, the stars were just as powerful deities as Jupiter, Isis, and Cybele, and magic as efficacious a way of getting one's wishes satisfied as ritual or prayer.

The superstition par excellence of the age was astrology. Its ultimate source was Babylon, where long ago court astronomers had built up an archive of celestial observations. The Babylonians had come to the conclusion that there was an all-encompassing Fate ruling stars and earth and man, that Fate had built in a correspondence between the movements in heaven and those on earth, including man's, and that, inasmuch as the movements of heavenly bodies were fixed, so were those of earthly bodies, and thus men's lives were inexorably determined by the movements of heavenly bodies. For any person on earth they could foretell whether he would joyfully be thanking his lucky stars or sorrowfully discovering he was star-crossed (the effects have permeated our very language).

Greek intellectuals as early as Plato and Aristotle's successor, Theophrastus, had heard about astrology, but it was not until Alexander's conquest of Babylon that the infection was released upon the Greek world. By the second century B.C. a subcenter of astrological lore had been established at Alexandria, and from this teeming entrepôt, where so many trade routes converged, astrologers carried their message to the four corners of the Roman world. In the version worked out for the new audience, the seven planets were equated with traditional Greek gods, each was given a color, plant, mineral, even a vowel from the Greek alphabet, to be its symbols, and each was assigned its special influence upon the lives of men. After the planets, the twelve signs of the zodiac.

The eternal seductiveness of astrology needs no discussion. What is somewhat startling is the universality of its appeal in Roman times, its strength within every social stratum, including the very highest—the emperors themselves not only believed but made public display of their belief. Augustus issued coins stamped with the sign under which he was born, Capricorn. When Tiberius retired to spend his last years at a villa on Capri, among the intellectuals he chose to have about him was one of the most famous astrologers of the day. Domitian minted a coin to commemorate his infant son's death, showing the babe seated on the globe of the earth stretching out his hands toward the seven planets. A bust of Commodus rests upon a sphere whose reliefs bear the three signs of the zodiac that governed the most important days of his life. Both Augustus and Tiberius banned astrologers from Rome at one time or another—not, of course, to rid the capital of frauds but in fear of subversion from rivals whose horoscopes might have told them that their ascent to the throne was in the stars.

Fate and the stars can be a grim and depressing burden: what is the sense of initiative or action if the events of one's life are spelled out in advance as inexorably as the movements of the heavenly bodies? What joy is there in living under such a sword of Damocles? Lucian, whose voice of reason rings out with blessed clarity amid the mumbo jumbo of this age, in one of his imaginary dialogues set in the underworld, has a pirate newly dead and standing for judgment before the awful Minos defend himself on the grounds that not he but the irresistible ordinances of Fate were responsible for his wrongdoings. Carneades, head of the philosophical school of skepticism in the second century B.C., asked how it was that men fated to die at different times went down in the same shipwreck. But Carneades' acute criticisms and Lucian's mockery were feeble things against the tide of unreason. The astrologers had their solution to offer: by knowing precisely what the stars had in store, one could arrange somehow to outwit them. And so there was a rush to patronize the horoscope casters, from Tiberius's learned companion on Capri to the itinerants who canvassed illiterate village folk and were responsible for the scribbled horoscopes that archaeologists have found in the rubbish heaps of Egypt. Or people renewed their prayers in the sanctuaries of Isis or Serapis or Mithras and other gods whose power presumably transcended the stars, who could grant their worshipers release; "I alone may prolong the span of life allotted by Fate" was Isis's boast. Or they turned to an equally potent form of superstition—magic.

Magic's virtue is that its realm is unbounded. With the right formulas, the right incantations, the right gestures, a man can force even the stars to bend to his will. Moreover, it is quick: you do not have to spend long hours in prayer and then hope the god will be persuaded; you invoke the demon who, again through the medium of appropriate words and actions, will be constrained to act in your behalf. Here, for example, is the magic to catch a thief; it was written sometime during the fourth century A.D. on a piece of papyrus paper found in Egypt:

I call thee, Hermes, immortal god, who cuttest a furrow down Olympus . . . the great, everliving, terrible to behold and terrible to be heard, give up the thief whom I seek. *Aberamentho oulerthe xenax sonelueothnemareba.* This spell is to be said twice at the purification. The spell of bread and cheese. Come to me, *lisson maternamau, erte, preptektioun, intiki, ous, olokotous, periklusai,* bring to me that which is lost, and make the thief manifest on this very day. And I invoke Hermes, the discoverer of thieves, and the sun and the eye-pupils of the sun, the two bringers-to-light of unlawful deeds, and Justice, and Erinys, and Ammon, and Parammon, to seize the throat of the thief and to manifest him this day, at the present hour.

We quote in the next chapter a formula for putting a hex on a rival racing team. Magic, as just mentioned, is unlimited; it can aim at the highest targets as well as the lowly. When Tiberius's nephew, Germanicus, died of illness in Syria in A.D. 19, a search of his room, Tacitus reports, revealed "the remains of human bodies, spells, curses, lead tablets inscribed with Germanicus's name, ashes half-burned and smeared with gore, and other evil devices by which souls are believed to be doomed to the shades of the Underworld."

Astrology was by no means the only way to know the future. One could do it as well through the correct interpretation of dreams, since these were assumed to be divinely inspired. Men took them as seriously as horoscopes. A certain Artemidorus from Asia Minor toward the end of the second century A.D. wrote a book on the subject that has survived, a catalogue of everything anyone could possibly dream of (and lots that no one ever would) with an interpretation of each, a veritable encyclopedia of balderdash. Then there were the oracles. Some were hoary and respected institutions, like that of Apollo at Delphi or Zeus at Dodona. Heads of nations used to consult them, and the priests in charge were capable of issuing statesmanlike advice or framing answers that were masterfully ambiguous. But in the time of the Roman Empire most had degenerated to the level of the palm or tea-leaf reader. One of the pieces of scrap paper unearthed from Egypt's rubbish heaps is a list of the standard questions addressed by visitors to an oracle; here is a sampling:

No. 73: Am I to remain where I am going?
No. 74: Am I to be sold?
No. 75: Am I to receive help from my friend?
No. 76: Has it been granted to me to make a contract with another person?
No. 77: Am I to be reconciled with my offspring?
No. 78: Am I to get a furlough?
No. 79: Am I to get the money?

Obviously the seer took on all comers—slaves, soldiers, businessmen, distracted parents. Lucian tells the story of a gifted quack who actually created a highly successful oracle from scratch in a backwater on the south shore of the Black Sea. There, for stiff prices, a talking serpent he had rigged up answered questions for the local hayseeds and was so successful that

the fame of the shrine made its way to Italy and descended on Rome. Every soul there, one on the heels of the other, hurried either to go out in person or to send an envoy, particularly the most influential and important personages in the city. The leader and prime figure in this movement was Rutilianus [a prominent Roman]. . . . He heard about the shrine and practically threw up his current public office to fly off to Abonoteichos; as next best thing he sent out one envoy after another. . . . He got the people at the emperor's court so worked up, most of them promptly rushed out to hear something about their own futures.

Rutilianus was no worse than his compeers. Pliny the Younger comforted his good friend Suetonius by interpreting his dreams. Suetonius needed it; his superstition knew no bounds. It was he who reports with dismay Caesar's cynical disregard of a fortuneteller's warning to beware the Ides of March, who gives us an endless catalogue of the portents that accompanied the birth, acts, and death of the emperors whose biographies he wrote.

From the east came not only Cybele, Isis, Mithras, mystery cults, astrology, and magic, but also the religion that was eventually to absorb and supplant them all—Christianity.

It offered a Savior who did not belong to a remote past but whose teaching and miracles were within living memory. It offered a message of hope not only for those who could afford an initiation or a costly sacrificial victim but for all, including the destitute, the derelict, the criminal. It insisted on a rite that was simple and clean and uplifting, not designed to overawe or morbidly excite. Like the Jewish faith from which it sprang, it was proudly exclusive: the worshiper of Christ would not include other deities in his prayers or bend his knees to the image of a Roman emperor.

The early Christians clashed with pagan authorities as inevitably as had the Jews, and during the period we are surveying they suffered frequent and cruel persecution. But the future was theirs. Wtihin two centuries Isis had succumbed to the Virgin Mary, Asclepius and Serapis had yielded their powers to healing saints, and architects were building churches with columns cannibalized from Apollo's or Jupiter's crumbling temples.

CHAPTER X

Fun and Games

"Serve him wine and dice," calls the tavernkeeper to a waiter in a little poem attributed to Vergil. The two went naturally together: dice and knucklebones (four- instead of six-sided pieces) were to the Roman what playing cards are to us, an important feature of daily life, a pleasant and cheap and convenient means for whiling away spare time. The ancient artist drew men absorbed in a dice game, just as Cézanne drew card players. Augustus enjoyed dice so much that he allowed play during his dinner parties—and, being a considerate host as well as a skilled crapshooter, deliberately lost, since he otherwise would have cleaned his guests out. Claudius had a special carriage fitted with a gaming board. And, as we all know, when Caesar made the most momentous move of his career, he used an expression from the gaming table: "The die is cast."

In addition to the various versions of throwing dice, the Romans went in for the games that use them to move counters on a board. Rich men had expensive tables fitted for the two board games that were most popular, just as people today include chess or checker tables among their furnishings. We find game boards scratched in the steps of public buildings or on the paving of public squares—places where people would wait around or tend to gather. Though the games were pastimes, they were treated as seriously as we treat chess or bridge. The story is told of a philosopher condemned to death who was ahead in a game with a fellow prisoner just when the sentry came to fetch him for execution; he insisted that the sentry check the board in case his opponent tried to claim a victory after he was gone.

Sports, then as now, were another favored way of filling one's moments of leisure. The Romans inherited all the varieties that the Greeks had introduced and made popular—boxing, wrestling, track, field, various types of ball playing. There was one game resembling handball (it involved hitting a ball against a wall) that seems to have been for the Romans what tennis is for us. Public baths often had courts for this game and so did private villas; Pliny had them at both his seashore and country villas.

Then there were the organized public sports, the equivalent of our professional baseball or football.

Rome's first festivals were connected with agriculture, honoring gods of the fields and crops. Though they continued to be celebrated by country folk more or less throughout Roman history, they meant little to the city dweller. What absorbed his interest was a series of festivals called *ludi*, "games," which had been established over the years to mark notable happenings. The Ludi Megalenses, a seven-day holiday from April 4 to 10, honored the Great Mother goddess who had brought victory over Hannibal; the Ludi Apollinares, lasting from July 6 to 13, thanked Apollo for his help with a plague (as well as invoking such help in all future plagues), and so on. In the imperial period, the emperors steadily introduced others to commemorate their own accomplishments, such as the Ludi Augustales, a ten-day holiday in honor of Augustus that was first celebrated in 11 B.C. and was made annual after his death. At the end of the second century B.C. there were six *ludi*, four of which lasted five to eight days, and two fourteen and fifteen for a total of fifty-seven days annually; by Augustus's time additions had raised this figure to seventy-seven, and by the second century A.D., very likely to more than one hundred. The programs of the *ludi* offered two forms of entertainment that are rarely put together, theatre and horse racing. The first was given the lion's share of time; the second was reserved for an all-day grand finale, except in the longer festivals where it extended over three to five days. The *ludi* were official occasions, run and paid for by the government, so entrance was free—if one could get one's hands on a ticket, which was not always easy. In the theatres, the best seats, right in front of the stage, were reserved for senators and visiting dignitaries, fourteen front rows for the next highest social class, and everyone else had to scramble for what was left. Women and men were seated separately. The magistrates in charge of public entertainment signed a contract with the manager of a troupe of actors, or with an acting star, to supply a given number of performances, and with the racing stables to supply a given number of teams, chariots, and drivers.

The theatrical entertainment, although, thanks to tradition, it absorbed more than two-thirds of the time available, was the less important. In the days of the republic, the programs ran heavily to tragedy and comedy, even high comedy; this was when Plautus and Terence made their reputations. But Roman dramatic taste was never very cultivated, and in the period that most concerns us, the preferred fare was what the ancients called mime. Although no examples of Roman mimes have survived, many of their titles have, and from these and random remarks dropped by ancient writers it is clear that they were a form of burlesque skit, swift-moving one-act affairs that used the time-honored ingredients of surprise (for example, a standard plot was *modo egens repente dives,* "now a pauper and suddenly wealthy," or "rags to riches in a day"), violence (in a mime about the life of the Roman equivalent of Jesse James, he ends up being crucified on stage and vomiting blood all about), and above all sex, with emphasis on adultery and the time-honored trinity of smooth lover, artful wife, and duped husband. In ancient tragedy and comedy it was fixed tradition for actors to be masked and for all parts to be played by men; Roman mimes were the sole exception: for more realistic effect, masks were dispensed with, and women played the female roles—which in some pieces involved stripping on stage.

Another form of entertainment that found as much favor as the mime was the vaudeville act: tumblers and tight-rope walkers and other acrobats, jugglers, magicians, puppeteers, performing animals. The last were so popular that when an audience was bored with what they were seeing, the standard cry was "Bring on a bear!" Only one highbrow type of performance was encouraged, the pantomime, a combination of mime—our kind—and ballet. It was almost always done by a single performer, usually male, wearing an elegant form of mask and dressed in elaborate costume. While a chorus sang about some mythological or historical event—as one ancient critic put it, the subjects could include anything from the primal Chaos to Cleopatra—the pantomimist danced it out, telling its story through steps, gestures, expressive movements of every part of his body. By means of rapid-fire changes of mask, he would dance a whole series of such stories. Pantomime stars commanded followings as devoted as those of today's pop singers. Order in the theatre was maintained by a unit of the city's daytime police force; when Nero once removed them as an enlightened public gesture, brawling between the adherents of rival artists became so serious that he quickly had to put the men back on duty.

As might be expected, the theatre had scant social standing. The actors were practically all foreigners, mostly Greeks, many of whom had started as slaves. Only a handful who rose to stardom and could command huge prices for their performances were able to break the barriers; they amassed enormous fortunes, and under culturally minded emperors such as Nero or Hadrian, they even gained acceptance at court. Some were women, for a career in the theatre was one of the few ways in which women could rise to prominence. The most spectacularly successful was the striptease queen Theodora, who ended up marrying the emperor Justinian.

Horse racing, although assigned much less time in the festival programs than the theatrical offerings, was the Roman spectator sport par excellence, outdrawing even the notorious gladiatorial combats. Juvenal growled in a celebrated phrase that the populace of Rome had only two things on its mind, "bread and circuses"; the circuses were the horse races. The favored racetrack was the Circus Maximus, which held a quarter of a million people, almost ten times as many as the combined capacity of Rome's three theatres, five times as many as that of the Colosseum. Stuffy intellectuals like Pliny the Younger might turn their noses up at the sport, but the rest of the population, all levels, went for it heart and soul—the emperors, with rare exceptions, were devoted fans, fashionable ladies considered attendance a must, and Trimalchio's cook was ready to lay a bet with his master on who was going to win.

The Greeks, from whom the Romans got the sport, included in their games racing both with chariots and on horseback (as today, except that they rode bareback and without stirrups). The Romans limited themselves to chariots. During the *ludi* twenty-four races were run a day, each consisting of seven laps, or about five miles, lasting some fifteen tense minutes. The main event was a race of four-horse teams; we hear of bigger teams, up to ten-horse, but they were not common, while beginners were allowed to drive two-horse teams. There could be as few as three teams in a race or as many as twelve; in a full field, with chariots riding wheel to wheel and the danger of collision and death ever present, spectators enjoyed all the thrills of the Indianapolis Speedway and of the sport of kings.

There were four great racing stables in Rome, each distinguished by a color, the Greens, Blues, Whites, and Reds. The Greens for some reason seem to have been the favorites: their adherents covered the social spectrum from emperors down to Trimalchio's cook, and, according to Juvenal, on a day when they lost, the gloom around town was deeper than when Rome suffered the worst military defeat in its history. The stables had headquarters in the city and, very probably, paddocks and other facilities outside. The staffs, mostly slaves and freedmen, were large and specialized, including, besides the drivers, trainers, grooms, harness makers, supply clerks, doctors, veterinarians, and even waiters, since the headquarters buildings boasted dining rooms. The horses came from all over, but most and the best from North Africa and Spain. They were rigorously cared for, trained, and kept under tight guard, since fixing races is by no means a modern invention. (It goes back at least to the time when Pelops, Zeus's grandson, bribed an opponent's driver into loosing a chariot wheel so it would come off during one of the laps.) Some tried to ensure a win by casting spells: "I conjure you up, holy beings and holy names! Give your help to this spell and bind, enchant, hinder, strike, overturn, conspire against, destroy, kill, shatter Eucherius, the charioteer, and all his horses tomorrow in the circus at Rome. Let him not break well from the starting gate, nor race quickly, nor pass anyone. . . . " Spells had the advantage of being cheaper than bribery, if not as effective. Caligula, on whom ancient writers liked to pin every vice known to man, was accused of poisoning any horses and drivers who appeared to have a chance to defeat his beloved Greens.

At the racetrack, unlike the theatre, women and men sat together; Ovid, in his manual on how to make love, offers advice on picking up a girl there. Since betting was off-track as well as on, word of the winners was spread as quickly as possible. Pliny the Younger's uncle tells in his encyclopedia of an enterprising stable owner who used carrier swallows with legs the color of the victorious team to bring the news to Volterra, his home town, some 175 miles northwest of Rome. Successful drivers earned fabulous amounts. We know this from monuments they erected to themselves on which they proudly had inscribed the record of their achievements. One driver lists 1,462 first places in a career that lasted some 25 years. He averaged better than 170 races annually, with 100 victories in his best year, and his prizes totaled nearly 4 million sesterces, some $16 million.

Horse racing and theatrical entertainment, constituting the program of the *ludi,* the official games, were recurrent annual events. Gladiatorial contests, on the other hand, were offered only on given occasions; we have already noted at Pompeii the announcements for them on the walls. The organization and training of gladiators was originally run by private businessmen, who often gave the shows as well. However, at Rome in our period it had all been taken over by the government. The emperors felt that gladiators were too dangerous an instrument to leave in other hands; the revolt of Spartacus, though it had happened long before, in 73–71 B.C., had by no means faded from people's memories. Augustus in his will records that he had sponsored gladiatorial exhibitions eight times, involving 10,000 pairs of fighters. Titus inaugurated the opening of the Colosseum in A.D. 80 with 100 consecutive days of contests. Audiences had a veritable glut when Trajan celebrated the successful close of one of his military campaigns with 123 days, involving 10,000 gladiators and 11,000 wild animals.

The Colosseum was the last word in amphitheatres. Beneath the level of the arena was a rabbit warren of cages for wild animals and dressing rooms for contestants. The stands accommodated fifty thousand; they included a special box for the emperor, reserved front rows for magistrates, foreign dignitaries, and senators, reserved rows behind them for the next highest social class, blocks of seats set aside for soldiers, priests, and other groups. Women were not only segregated from the men, as in the theatre, but consigned to the worst seats in the house, at the very top; the priggish Augustus even barred them when the program included sports contests, since athletes performed in the nude. Back of the women's rows was standing room for the poverty-stricken with no claim to any of the seats. The whole area was shaded from the sun by canvas awnings so vast and complicated that a unit of sailors from the imperial navy was stationed in Rome to operate them. The safety precautions were airtight. The seating area was effectively sealed off by barriers, and there were rotating cylinders set at the base of the stands so that, in the rare event of a frenzied animal being able to vault the barriers, it could not get the footing for a leap into the spectators' midst.

The Romans inherited gladiatorial combats, along with so much else, from their northern neighbors, the Etruscans. This gifted and aggressive people actually ruled Rome for a time and remained its most dangerous neighbor until they were finally conquered shortly after 300 B.C. One of their religious practices was the holding of a duel to the death between two armed men beside a tomb of a chief whose spirit required a sacrifice of blood. In the third century B.C. the Romans introduced such duels as part of the ceremonies honoring the death of great leaders—but with no religious content, merely as an addition to the program that was sure to find favor with the audience. By the first century B.C. these had developed into not only a form of entertainment pure and simple, but one so popular that it proved a profitable form of investment. The owner of a troupe of gladiators (they were originally all slaves) contracted with the magistrates in charge of public entertainment or with private producers to furnish fighters at a fixed fee per head plus payment of a lump sum for any who were killed. Cicero's good friend Atticus, a multimillionaire and canny financier, owned a troupe, and so did Caesar; his establishment, located in Capua, was equipped to handle no less than 5,000 gladiators. Thus, when the emperors decided that it was more prudent and useful to handle the sport themselves, they merely had to take over going concerns.

The head of a gladiatorial school, called a *lanista,* acquired his gladiators in a number of ways. Some he got from the state, which had adopted the practice of condemning certain criminals to the gladiator barracks instead of the mines or exile; men so condemned had to put in three years in the arena. Others were slaves he purchased on the market, most often prisoners of war or victims of kidnapping and piracy. Still others were slaves sold to him by masters who wanted to get rid of them; Hadrian, however, limited these to slaves who either consented (presumably they considered the rewards worth the risk) or had committed some offense. All served until they were freed in response to the acclamation of the crowd after a brilliant fight or had earned enough money in prizes to buy their liberty. Lastly, a *lanista* could count on the services of a good number who were free men to start with and signed on either under the pressure of debt or simply for the joy of fighting and the chance it gave to become a public figure; a successful gladiator made as good money and received as much adulation as today's baseball and football stars. The profession was not limited to men; combats between women also found a place on the programs.

A recruit, or *tiro,* as he was called, began his training by hacking with a wooden sword on wooden dummies under the eye of skilled coaches, either experienced or retired gladiators. Beginners all went through this course, and on the basis of it, were then assigned to the various specialties. Tough, heavy men were trained to be *Galli* or *mirmillones,* who fought in a full suit of armor with shield and sword of standard size. Lighter, quicker men became *Thraces,* who fought with light armor, buckler, and short curved sword. Those who were lightning quick were trained to be *retiarii,* "net men." The *retiarius,* wearing only a tunic and armed with but a trident, dagger, and net, faced a heavy-armed gladiator; victory depended on a single cast of the net—if he caught his opponent in its toils, he was the winner, if not, it was all over. Still others learned to fight from horseback and chariots.

The men did not lead an austere barracks existence. Many were married with children. They had affairs with women—indeed, they were reputed to be well-nigh irresistible to the loose ladies of Roman high society. On the wall of the house in Pompeii where a group of gladiators lived one *Thrax* scribbled that he was the *suspirium puellarum,* "what the girls sighed for."

The duelists in gladiatorial combats were usually mixed to avoid monotony: heavy-armed fought against light-armed and *retiarii* as well as other heavy-armed; light-armed fought against heavy-armed as well as other light-armed. When a contestant had fallen and lay as if dead, an attendant rushed out with a hot iron to make sure he was not bluffing, stretcher-bearers hauled the corpse away, other attendants spread clean sand to cover the blood (the word *arena* means "sand" in Latin), and the next match went on. In republican times, when the sport was still in private hands, programs were run in which the duels were to the death, but under the empire this was abolished. They might end in a draw, or a man who was clearly losing could appeal for mercy; it was then up to the magistrate running the show, and he generally followed the crowd's wishes. They waved handkerchiefs or turned their thumbs downward if they judged the pleader had fought bravely and deserved to be spared, turned their thumbs against their chests if they judged otherwise. It appears that gladiators usually fought once a year, or even less. We deduce this from the inscriptions that they, like chariot drivers, set up in their own honor with the details of their careers. Quite a few list thirty fights or more, indicating a fair survival rate.

Gladiatorial Games Scene. A wild animal is let loose on a helpless victim.
Third century A.D. Mosaic from El Djem, Tunisia.

The duels between gladiators, although cruel and bloody, at least
involved a display of skill, as well as a good chance of coming out alive.
But there were two other items on the program before them—the
gladiators went on in the afternoon—that could end in nothing but
death.

The state condemned men convicted of serious crimes not merely
"to the gladiator school" but "to the sword" or "to the beasts" and
handed them over at so much per head to the magistrate in charge of
gladiatorial shows; he guaranteed to leave them corpses within a year
from the date of purchase. At a given point in the program, generally at
noon before the gladiatorial combats proper, they were thrust into the
arena either in a helpless herd to be butchered by gladiators or tied to
stakes to be attacked by wild beasts who had been kept in a state of near
starvation.

For this slaughter there may perhaps be the pallid excuse that the
Romans, having judged the victims to be brutal criminals, saw no
wrong in a brutal execution, and, as we know from the reports of

attendance at hangings or guillotinings, all the world loves an execution. But for the morning portion of a program at the amphitheatre, there was not even this much. At vast expense the Roman government imported animals from every corner of the known world—tigers from India, leopards from Asia Minor, lions and elephants and other creatures from Africa, wild bulls from northern Europe, and so on. They were kept in cages under the arena until, at the appropriate moment, they were brought up and let loose. As they wandered about, crazed or dazed, *bestiarii,* "beast men," low-level gladiators trained for this sort of thing, stepped in against them with knife and spear; the *bestiarius* had a chance of surviving, the animals none. Or crack native hunters were sent in to cut them down ruthlessly with bow and arrow or javelin— which at least added some dimension of skill to the carnage. It went on endlessly. During the 100 days of gladiatorial shows that inaugurated the Colosseum, 9,000 beasts were killed; during Trajan's 123 days to honor his military victory, 11,000.

Throughout the western half of the empire and even in parts of the east, every community had its amphitheatre for these bloody programs. In many cases the ruins are still visible; not a few have been refurbished and are again in use, by the *bestiarius*'s direct heir, the bullfighter. Intellectuals like Cicero or Marcus Aurelius were bored or disgusted with what went on in the arena, moralists like Seneca deplored it, but the first concerted protest came from the Christians—and they were not opposed to the brutality per se but to all sights they considered degrading; they clamored equally loudly against the theatre and circus. Ultimately, in A.D. 325, Constantine issued a decree forbidding gladiatorial combats. But the sport was far too popular to be canceled by the stroke of a pen, and it lingered on for at least a century more. The slaughter of wild beasts did not come under the ban. That lasted as long as ancient Rome did.

CHAPTER XI

On the Road

Sometime in the second century A.D. an Alexandrian businessman wrote from Rome to his brother in Egypt as follows: "I am well. This is to let you know that I reached land on Epeiph 6 [June 30] and we unloaded our cargo on the 18th of the same month. I went up to Rome [from the port at the mouth of the Tiber] on the 25th of the same month [July 19]. . . . We are daily expecting our sailing papers; up to today not one of the grain freighters has been cleared. Remember me to your wife and dear ones." There were enough ships in that fleet of carriers to transport 135,000 tons of Egyptian wheat annually. Wheat from Egypt, olive oil from Spain, wine from France, carved stone coffins from Athens—these and dozens of other products were hauled back and forth across the Mediterranean by a merchant marine larger than any Europe was to know again till the eighteenth century. Traders used the roads as well, but to a much smaller extent, since carriage on land was either by donkey or oxcart, both as expensive as they were slow. The roads in the first instance had been built for the government, and the officers of the government remained their chief user on a regular basis.

Nor did trade stop at the boundaries of the empire. The Roman upper classes had developed a taste for exotic luxuries, and during the peaceful and prosperous first two centuries of the Christian era they had the money to indulge it. The shippers of Alexandria sent long fingers of trade down the east coast of Africa as far as Zanzibar and across the sea to India; from the one they brought back ivory and myrrh, from the other spices and cotton fabrics, as well as silk that had been shipped there from China.

The demand for silk, that luxury of luxuries, became so avid that it finally brought into contact the two great civilizations of the ancient world, Greco-Roman and Chinese. In the second century B.C. China began dispatching silk caravans on a more or less regular schedule from within the Great Wall deep into Chinese Turkestan. There the loads were transferred to local middlemen who carried them across the desert and through the mountains to Persia, where Syrians and Greeks took them over for the last leg to the Mediterranean. In A.D. 97 the court of China sent an envoy, Kan Ying, to Mesopotamia; he or a successor reported back that the people there were "honest in their transactions, and there are no double prices"—probably the first and last time that has been said about Near Eastern tradesmen. Groups of Greco-Roman merchants made their way into China, for the court records report that in "the ninth year of the Yen-hsi period, during the Emperor Huan-ti's reign [A.D. 166] . . . the king of Ta-ts'in, Antun, sent an embassy which, from the frontier of Jih-nan [Annam], offered ivory, rhinoceros horns, and tortoise shell." The account goes on to comment sniffily that the embassy had brought the emperor no jewels. Ta-ts'in is the Chinese name for the Roman Empire, and An-tun is Antoninus, the family name of Marcus Aurelius, but what arrived was almost certainly no official body, simply a clutch of traders attempting to buy their silk directly from China instead of through middlemen.

But trade and the government were by no means responsible for all the movement on the roads and sea lanes. There were plenty of people on the go for other reasons.

To begin with, there were those traveling for their health, headed for a sanctuary of the healing god Asclepius. These centers were to be found all over Greece, on the islands of the eastern Mediterranean, in the Greek cities along the coast of Asia Minor, in those of southern Italy. As early as 291 B.C. one had been established on the Tiber Island in Rome. In the days of the empire, three had become the most prestigious: those at Epidaurus in Greece, on the island of Kos, where Hippocrates had been born and founded his school of medicine, and at Pergamum; this last reached its height in the middle of the second century A.D. when Galen, the most renowned physician of the day, practiced there, on and off, for many years. The procedure was the same in all. The patients entered the sanctuary, took a ritual bath to purify themselves, went into Asclepius's temple, prayed, and then spread a pallet and lay down on it to spend the night. Their dreams revealed to them the help they sought. In a few notable cases the cures were miraculous: the patients awoke the next morning hale and hearty. More often they were given some prescription, usually spelled out plainly, occasionally enigmatically. There was rarely anything exotic about these; for the most part they involved the taking—or not taking—of certain baths or exercise or foods, applications of unguents and salves, downing of doses of special drugs.

Asclepius's ministrations were for the severely ill. For the merely ailing and particularly the hypochondriacs, there were the *aquae,* the mineral springs. These were as well patronized in Roman days as European spas in our own; in some cases one is the descendant of the other. Aquae Calidae has become Vichy, Aquae Sextiae Aix-en-Provence, Aquae Sulis Bath, and so on. Their ancient clientele was every bit as sure they did one good as today's is. "Many throughout Sicily," wrote Diodorus, a contemporary of Caesar and Augustus, "who are troubled with their peculiar ills go [to Lipari] . . . and by using the baths become healthy again in incredible fashion."

Then there were the crowds en route to the great festivals that had achieved international repute. The traditional Greek games, the Olympics in honor of Zeus or the Pythian in honor of Apollo, lasted almost as long as the Roman Empire itself. And out-of-towners must have poured into Rome by the thousands when the *ludi* were on or gladiatorial shows were being given, and by the tens of thousands for such events as the opening of the Colosseum.

Lastly we must add the vacationers, all those who could afford to flee the heat of the cities during the summer for the cool of the sea or the mountains. Rome's upper crust started the annual migration at the coming of spring. Since the resort hotel was unknown in ancient times, they moved from one to another of their private villas. Cicero, merely a moderately wealthy man by the standards of his day, had no less than six: three along or near the lovely Bay of Naples, one on the coast north of there, and two in the hills not far from Rome. His neighbors along the Bay of Naples included some of the greatest names in Roman history— Julius Caesar, Mark Antony, the celebrated *bon vivant* Lucullus, among others—whose establishments put his to shame. Augustus's stepfather owned one where he once entertained not only Caesar but Caesar's retinue of two thousand. The most stupendous of all was the villa Lucullus built at Naples—and he had another, only slightly less sumptuous, just twelve miles to the west. Augustus maintained at least four in the area. His successor Tiberius spent most of the last ten years of his life at a monumental establishment on Capri. Nero was staying at his villa at Baiae, on the western arm of the bay, the night he attempted to drown his mother; he finally had her assassinated in the bedroom of her own place a few miles away. Baiae, as a matter of fact, was one of the favored spots; with its abundant hot springs, it was spa as well as summer resort. The villas of the wealthy lined the shores and spangled the hills roundabout, while in town were rooms and lodgings for the rank and file. Pleasure seekers of all kinds flocked there and, as will happen, gave the town a reputation for impure as well as pure delights. The respectable elements of society sailed decorously on the nearby Lake Lucrinus during the day; at night the smart set invited shady women aboard their yachts, went bathing in the nude, and "filled the lakes with the din of their singing." "Unmarried girls are common property, old men act like young boys, and lots of young boys like young girls," snapped Varro, Cicero's learned contemporary. "Why must I look at drunks staggering along the shore or noisy boating parties?" complained the moralist

Seneca a century later. Who wants to listen, he grumbled, "to the squabbles of nocturnal serenaders?" Martial composed a sardonic little poem about a certain couple, of whom

> The wife, even worse than her glowering husband
>   never strayed from virtue's paths,
> until she came to the Lucrine Lake
>   and heated up in Baiae's baths.
> It put her on fire: she left him flat
>   to run off with some young boy;
> she came to town Penelope,
>   she left it Helen of Troy.

The straitlaced Augustus, though he often vacationed in his villas in the neighborhood, never showed his face in town and took a dim view of those who did.

With the onset of the heat in May, Rome's high society left their seaside establishments and moved to the cool of the hills. The Alban and Sabine hills that ring Rome on the east and southeast were dotted with country retreats. In the neighborhood of Tusculum alone there were four belonging to various emperors and ten times that many to private citizens. For in the prosperous years of the Roman Empire, this sort of indulgence was not limited to the wealthy; the middle class as well had country refuges. The farm in the Sabine hills that Horace got from his patron Maecenas, where he rushed gratefully on every possible occasion, was no grandiose villa but a modest bit of land with a modest rustic-style house. Martial, who started his career living in a garret three flights up, eventually acquired a little cottage surrounded by a few acres some thirteen miles as the crow flies from where Horace's had been located. Though we call these establishments farms, many were as purely ornamental as the glamorous estates of the millionaires. Martial pokes fun at a second-rate lawyer who made a poor but sure living off a clientele who paid him in produce—until he bought a piece of farm property to retire on, and then things suddenly were reversed:

So, Pannychus, you've bought some land
    with a ramshackle hut whose roof needs supports,
with a view on a roadside graveyard, and
    you've deserted your city estate, the courts.

Your seedy gown paid steadily, if not well—
    but the millet, barley, wheat, and rye,
that when practicing law you used to sell,
    now you're a farmer, you'll have to buy!

When the owners of such "farms" set out for a weekend in the country, they had to carry their own food with them. Take the one that Martial saw on the Appian Way in a cart groaning under a load of cabbages, leeks, lettuce, fowl, and so on:

Is he homeward bound
    from the country air?
It's the other way round—
    he's going there!

To go by sea or by land—this was the first issue a traveler had to resolve. In most cases the choice was simple: he favored travel by sea over land as much as we do travel by air over the train; it spared him long, scorching days in a jolting carriage or on shanks' mare. Since there were no regular passenger lines, he would make his way to the nearest port and patiently put up there until he found a freighter headed to where he wanted to go, preferably one of the big merchantmen that hauled bulky commodities like grain and oil between distant ports. Running as much as 180 feet in length and able to carry a thousand tons of cargo and accommodate hundreds of passengers, they offered safety and, with their ample decks, relative comfort. Ancient freighters, even the largest, were equipped with only a handful of cabins for use by VIPs, friends of the owner or shipper, and such; anyone else, including well-heeled travelers, willy-nilly took deck passage. They came aboard carrying collapsible shelters, which they set up as sleeping quarters at night, carrying provisions for the length of the voyage, and accompanied by one or more servants—only paupers or fugitives traveled without at least one servant—to take care of the housekeeping involved. The ship supplied only drinking water. Since the sailing season was limited to the late spring, summer, and early fall, and since the Mediterranean climate is comparatively mild, deck passage was usually no great hardship. Neither was the length of the voyage. With just ordinary luck with the winds, ancient sailing vessels could get from Naples to Alexandria in two weeks, from Naples to Athens in a week, from Athens to the west coast of Asia Minor in a few days. However, because of the prevailing northerlies in the eastern Mediterranean, the voyage home was a much slower business; Alexandria back to Rome, for example, could take as much as two and a half months.

If his destination lay inland, the traveler came as near as he could by sea and then resigned himself to exchanging his comfortable spot on the deck for the rigors of the open road. During the first and second centuries A.D. land travel in one respect was better than it was to be at any subsequent time till the coming of the railroad: a web of paved, all-weather highways linked the farthest corners of the empire with the capital; rain simply made a traveler wet, it did not mire him for hours or days in a sea of mud. These splendid roads marched along, mile after mile, over open desert, along the shoulders of ravines, up to and across mountain passes. Strategically placed along the main routes were inns or posting stations where bed and food were to be had and beasts and vehicles could be hired. The beasts were generally donkeys or mules (horses, expensive to maintain, were for the army or races). The vehicles varied from light two-wheeled gigs for fast travel to heavy four-wheeled affairs with arched cloth or leather canopies looking very much like our Conestoga wagons. There was even a *carruca dormitoria,* a "sleeping carriage," the ancient equivalent of today's car trailer. None of them, light or heavy, offered any joy ride, since all had wooden wheels with iron tires and were innocent of springs. The wealthy, though they could do nothing about the discomfort of a ride, devised ingenious ways to mitigate its monotony. We have already mentioned Claudius's carriage fitted for shooting dice; Commodus had one equipped with swiveling seats, enabling him to catch the sun or a cooling breeze or merely change the view; Pliny's indefatigable uncle had one with room for a stenographer and his gear. Those who wanted to avoid being jounced about at all costs, and cared nothing about time or expense, used litters rather than carriages. The traveling litter was fitted with a canopy and draw curtains; the rider lolled on cushions in shaded ease as six or eight husky bearers plodded along, averaging fifteen to twenty miles a day. Ordinary carriage travel averaged twenty-five to thirty.

When night began to fall, the traveler hastened his pace to reach a city, or if he was in open country, the next roadside inn before dark. In either case, he was rather worse off than his counterpart today. The ancient world had nothing that we would dignify with the name "hotel"; there were only humble inns, which offered the very minimum in food and lodging and usually doubled as houses of ill repute. The rich arranged their itineraries so that they could either stay at their own country houses or be put up by friends or relatives; moreover, in case of need they could count on hospitality from local governors or mayors. "Lucius Memmius, a Roman senator in a position of considerable importance and honor," runs a letter penned in 112 B.C. by some clerk in Egypt's foreign office at Alexandria to the mayor of an Egyptian town, "is sailing [up the Nile] . . . to see the sights. Receive him in the grand style and see to it that, at the usual points, lodgings are prepared . . . and that the gifts, a list of which is attached below, are presented to him."

Those who were traveling on government business had the enormous advantage of having the facilities of the *cursus publicus,* the government post, available to them. This was another of the superbly useful pieces of Roman administrative machinery created by Augustus. It encompassed a network of more or less well equipped inns at given intervals all along the major routes with, in between, simple hostels that could take care of the minimum requirements—bed, a bite to eat, change of carriage or animals. The intervals depended on the terrain and on the density of population, but in general an effort was made to have inns available every twenty-five to thirty-five miles, that is, the length of an average day's travel. In between would be one or two hostels, again depending upon the terrain, more in mountainous areas, fewer on the flat. Hand lists were drawn up that detailed all the stopping places along the routes and the distances between them. There were also maps designed specifically to show not only the location of such places but what they had to offer. A copy made in the Middle Ages of one of these has survived, the so-called Tabula Peutingeriana. Done on an elongated parchment that is no more than thirteen inches wide but over twenty-two feet long, it presents a map of the Roman Empire as distorted as if seen in a trick mirror. The cartographer's aim was to give a schematic picture of the Roman road system in a form suitable for easy reference. There are lines showing routes; names of cities, towns, and other stopping places; numbers indicating the distance in Roman miles between them. Alongside many of the names stands a little colored picture symbol that, just like those in our guidebooks, shows at a quick glance the facilities afforded. A schematized picture of a four-sided building with a court in the center stands for an inn of some consequence, a picture of the front of a house with a twin-peaked roof for a less pretentious country inn, a single-peaked boxlike cottage for a very modest inn, and a name without any picture probably means that the simplest form of hostel was to be found there. Anyone carrying a *diploma,* a travel warrant signed by the emperor, would make his way, sleeping, eating, and picking up fresh vehicles and animals at the various inns and hostels, presumably in every instance the best the area boasted, at the government's expense.

The traveler without one of these magic pieces of paper had little choice: he might put up at one of the inns of the public post if its official guests had not exhausted its resources; otherwise he took whatever he could get. In either event it was not very much—most of the time a tiny cell of a room which might have to be shared with as many as half a dozen others and whose furnishings were generally limited to a bed, chair, and chamber pot. On occasion even some of these essentials were missing, as we gather from a message that an irate guest scratched on the wall of his room in an inn at Pompeii: "Innkeeper," he wrote, "I pissed on the bed. I did wrong, I admit it. Want to know why? There was no chamber pot!" The facilities for washing up were minimal, but at least in towns that was no problem since there were always the public baths.

Things were not much better when it came to meals. Ancient eating places, whether belonging to inns or independent establishments, were wine shops rather than restaurants, and more often than not, wine shops that catered to no very distinguished clientele—sailors, muleteers, slaves, the general run of street drifter. A traveler might send his servant out to buy food or might go himself to one of these eating places. If he was in a hurry he could stand at the snack bar, with its marble-topped counter that opened onto the street, and down his meal then and there. If he had more time and was not choosy about his dinner companions, he could walk through the shop to the rooms at the rear, where table service was provided. At counter or table he had to be on his guard to get his money's worth. The Roman physician Galen states bluntly that restaurateurs were not above using human flesh in their so-called pork roasts and stews. Whether this is true or not, there is no doubt whatsoever that overwatering the wine was a widespread malpractice; the ancients always added a certain amount of water to their wine, but unscrupulous innkeepers would put in more than the recipes called for. Martial, who spent a fair amount of time in Roman wine shops, has a number of pungent epigrams on the subject, for example:

> The rains this year left sopping wet
> the grapes on every vine.
> So, barkeep, don't you try to say
> there's no water in your wine.

Traders, officials, soldiers, throngs heading for a healing sanctuary or a festival, vacationers—all were on the road to accomplish something at the end of their journey. There was yet another form of traveler nourished by the long years of the Pax Romana, the one for whom the journey was its own end, the tourist. "Since many [these days go on voyages] and even set forth upon the seas to Egypt to visit the artistic creations of man," reads a papyrus found in Egypt, "I too made a

voyage." No longer, as in times past, did one have to be a monarch or
high dignitary or nobleman to afford such a pleasure. It lay within the
compass of many. Businessmen who had made their pile took the grand
tour, while traders found the time for trips to see the *notabilia* of the area
in which they happened to be, and functionaries those of the lands
where they were stationed.

What drew them to undertake the hardships of the road? Just as
today, it was above all else the magnetism of the relics of man's past. We
make the rounds of Europe's cathedrals, they made them of Greece's
temples. We trek to where Washington passed a night, where Napo-
leon's house stood, where Saint Paul was killed, where Saint Peter was
laid to rest; they trekked to where Alexander the Great passed a night,
where Socrates' house stood, where Ajax committed suicide, where
Achilles was buried. We make our way to famous galleries to view the
great art of the past; they went to famous temples, because the temples
of the ancient world doubled as museums. A temple in Asia Minor had
on display specimens of barbarian clothing, Indian amber, elephant
tusks; a temple of Apollo, god of healing, exhibited a special kind of
dentist's forceps; at Rome one could see Caesar's sword on view, appro-
priately enough, in the Temple of Mars, or the dagger that a would-be
assassin unsuccessfully tried to use on Nero displayed, equally appropri-
ately, in the Temple to the Goddess of Luck. We go to places where we
are solemnly shown splinters of the True Cross, the bottles in which
Lucretia Borgia kept her poisons, the very spot where Saint Paul's head
bounced three times after his decapitation; they went to where they
were shown the prow of Odysseus's ship, the very crag to which Zeus
chained Prometheus, the egg from which Helen of Troy was hatched
(Zeus had visited her mother in the form of a swan). We flock to
England for a visit to Shakespeare country; they flocked to Asia Minor
for a visit to Homer country, the site of Troy (the standard tour included the strip of beach along which the Greek ships had been pulled
up, the plain where Hector and Achilles had rampaged, the tomb of
Patroclus, the cave where Paris gave his fateful judgment, and so on). In
Egypt they went to see the same things we see today, the pyramids,

Sphinx, Valley of the Kings, and other testimonials to the greatness of the age of the pharaohs.

The ancient tourist did his sightseeing unencumbered by the miscellaneous gear that loads down his counterparts today (if he had anything to take along, the ubiquitous slave companion would do the carrying). He was not even burdened with a guidebook. Not that this most useful form of literature did not exist. From at least the second century B.C., there were available such titles as *The Athenian Acropolis, Spartan Cities,* and *Guidebook to Troy,* and in the second century A.D. Pausanias, the Karl Baedeker of the ancient world, published his excellent and detailed *Guidebook of Greece.* But these were for background reading; in any case, being handwritten on leather or papyrus like all ancient books, they were too valuable and bulky to lug around. As a consequence, the sightseer in Roman times was even more dependent on local guides than we are.

The chief problem was that, like their modern descendants, once launched on their patter they could not stop. "The guides went through their standard speech," grumbles one of the characters in a sketch Plutarch wrote about a group seeing the sights of Delphi, "paying no attention whatsoever to our entreaties to cut the talk short." A writer of satire has a character in one of his pieces pray fervently: "Zeus, protect me from your guides at Olympia, and you, Athena, from yours at Athens." It was not only that they never stopped talking; it was also what they talked about. They had the weakness, traditional in their profession, of preferring a gaudy tale to sober information. They particularly liked to connect whatever they were showing with the heroic days of mythological times, to point out the very spot on the road where Penelope had agreed to marry Odysseus, the very bones of a monster Hercules had killed, the very point on the beach where Aeneas had landed, and so on. "Abolish fabulous tales from Greece," snickered Lucian, "and the guides there would all die of starvation, since no tourist wants to hear the bald facts even for nothing."

The opportunity to see great works of art or historical buildings is what draws a tourist to a site. Once there, however, he enjoys diversion, welcomes any variation from the standard round of visiting churches, museums, and monuments. In ancient times as now, the locals had special performances to provide a change of pace for a footsore sightseer. One of the high points of the tour of the pyramids was to watch the men from a nearby village shinny up from the ground to the very tip— a real stunt in those days, when the sloping faces, with all their original stones intact, were absolutely smooth. Farther up the Nile, where the sacred crocodiles were kept, the priests had taught them to come when called and on command to open their jaws and let their teeth be cleaned.

The greatest performance of all, however, was put on by nature, not man. At Thebes in Egypt, not far from the Valley of the Kings, stands a colossal statue consisting of a base, a throne, and a seated male figure. We now know that it represents Pharaoh Amenhotep III, who reigned about 1400 B.C. The Greeks and Romans, however, preferred to believe it was a likeness of the mythological Memnon, child of the goddess of dawn. At some time, probably about 27 B.C., an earthquake broke the statue across the torso, and the upper part fell to the ground. The remainder developed a unique feature—the ability to utter sound. At daybreak—not any other time of day, only daybreak—it made what was described as a sharp cracking noise. The conviction arose, no doubt fostered by the local guides, that these sounds were Memnon's way of talking to his mother. There were some who looked for a rational explanation of the phenomenon, but in that age of rampant superstition they were voices in the wilderness. For the thousands who flocked there, the statue was actually talking. They kept flocking right up to the end of the second century A.D., when for some reason it shut up. Just about this time the emperor Septimius Severus had the piece that had fallen down replaced, and it may have been this that struck Memnon dumb. It has been suggested that the sound was caused by the sudden increase of temperature at sunrise, which heated air trapped in holes in the broken surface, causing it to expand and in escaping produce a sound. So, when the reconstruction covered up this surface the mysterious voice was abruptly silenced.

We know that those who were there took what was happening as a marvel because of another tourist characteristic that has not changed one whit during the course of the centuries—the compulsion to leave one's name in places one has been to. Almost the whole of Memnon's legs and base is covered with graffiti, over one hundred of them, the work of well-nigh two centuries of visitors whose ranks included eight governors of Egypt, three district governors, any number of army officers, two judges, a priest, even the empress Sabina, Hadrian's wife (though the emperor was there too, he did not inscribe, perhaps, as we gather from a graffito left by one of his entourage, because that day Memnon failed to perform). One, a self-styled "professor and poet," was so moved that he effused in verse:

He has learned to orate, he has learned to keep quiet;
    the force both of words and of silence he knows.
At the sight of the dawn, of his saffron-robed mother.
    he utters a sound, and more sweetly it flows
than the clearest of speech ever voiced by another.
This poem did Falernus, professor and poet, infuse
With a quality worthy of a Grace or a Muse.

Some others too were moved to verse, usually on the same near-doggerel level, but most contented themselves with a brief attestation of faith. "I heard the wonderful Memnon, along with my wife, Arsinoe," followed by the date and including the name, is typical.

Memnon, as Egypt's principal drawing card, boasts the greatest concentration of sightseers' graffiti. But there are plenty of others—in the tombs of the Valley of the Kings, on the Sphinx, the pyramids, the walls of various temples. The land of the Nile, it so happens, is where the bulk of them are found, but that is chiefly because the great tourist attractions in other parts of the ancient world—the Temple of Artemis at Ephesus, the statue of Zeus by Phidias at Olympia, and the like—have all completely disappeared.

Having visited the sights at a given place, witnessed whatever performances the locals had to offer, perhaps scratched his name, the ancient tourist was ready for that most gratifying of tourist activities, shopping.

Not too much information about ancient shopping is available, but there is enough to reveal that by and large only the objects of the hunt have changed, that the tastes and desires and purposes involved were much the same as now. The religious-minded Roman lady touring in Egypt brought back a container of Nile water to use in the service for Isis, just as the visitor to Italy today returns with a rosary. The amateur art lover came home from Athens with a replica in miniature of the great statue of Athena by Phidias, just as we come back from Florence with one of Michelangelo's *David*. Those who could afford it did not content themselves with miniatures; they ordered full-scale reproductions to adorn their town houses and country villas—a lucky thing for us, since the originals of most of the great Greek masterpieces have disappeared, and these copies are all that is left to show us what they were like. For those who just wanted a souvenir of a place, there were appropriate things available, as we can tell from specimens the archaeologists have dug up. In Afghanistan, for example, they found a glass vessel decorated with the scene of the harbor of Alexandria; surely it was taken to that far-off spot by some local who, having made the long trek to the great metropolis, wanted a memento of it. From Puteoli, the resort and port just north of Naples, come a number of examples of a typical tourist gimcrack—little glass flasks bearing a picture of the city's waterfront with the key sites identified by labels: "Lighthouse," "Nero's Pool," "The Oyster Beds," "Woods."

Very likely the ancient tourist shopped for locally available specialties. Anyone visiting Egypt had to pass through Alexandria and confronting him on all sides would be irresistible buys in products from Africa and the Far East. The traveler to Syria could pick up Syrian glass or Near Eastern carpets and embroidered textiles. In Asia Minor he could get fine woolens and linens. In Greece there were the excellent fabrics woven at Patras. If he got no farther than Athens, he could settle for a jar of the prized Mount Hymettus honey. We have only a very few vague references to the shopping habits of the Greek or Roman traveler, but they seem to indicate that he—or his wife—could no more pass up a bargain than we can. "If my health improves," writes a Greek living in Egypt to a friend, sometime in the third century B.C., "and I go abroad to Byzantium [the modern Istanbul], I'll bring you back some fine pickled fish." Both tuna and turbot were caught there, and either made as welcome a gift to someone living in second-century-B.C. Egypt as caviar or champagne to us.

There was one factor that must have held the shoppers' enthusiasm somewhat in check: the customs charges. The Roman Empire maintained stations not only at all ports and frontiers but also at the boundaries between provinces, since duty was payable even on goods crossing from one province to the next. Beasts of burden, wagons, luggage containers, and objects of personal use during the voyage were exempt. Everything else was dutiable—right down to corpses being transported for burial elsewhere. On most items the rate was not stiff, only 2 to 5 per cent ad valorem, but on the very things that tourists would find enticing, such as silks, perfumes, spices, pearls, and other exotic luxuries, it was a whopping 25 per cent.

However, as always, it helped to know the right people. "Send . . . a bathing costume as quickly as possible," runs a letter written in 257 B.C. by some person to the secretary of the minister of finance of Egypt, "preferably of goatskin or, if not, of sheepskin. Also a tunic and cloak and the mattress, blanket, pillows, and honey. You wrote me you were surprised that I didn't realize that all these items were subject to duty. I'm aware of it all right, but you are perfectly able to arrange to send them without any risk whatsoever."

CHAPTER XII

The Engineer

Strabo, the great Greek geographer, visited Rome several times in the last decades of the first century B.C. His examination of the city convinced him that

the Romans have made provision above all for those things that the Greeks have slighted: the construction of roads and aqueducts, and of sewers capable of washing away the city's waste into the Tiber. And they have laid roads throughout the country, cutting through hills and building up over valleys so that their wagons can carry veritable cargoes. Their sewers, covered with vaulting of cut stone, offer in places a channel haycarts could pass through. So much water is piped in through aqueducts that it flows like streams through the city and its drains.

The Romans, no question about it, were excellent engineers. Though the skill was all their own, they owed much of their know-how to their neighbors to the north, the Etruscans. The Etruscans were masters in the art of tunneling channels through rock—some of them run for over a mile and a half without a break—to carry off water or to bring it in. They covered the region they occupied with a network of fine roads, at times cutting great gashes fifty feet deep in stony hills to provide a gradient suitable for wheeled traffic. Rome's engineers for a long time simply carried on Etruscan methods. Not until the third century B.C. did they make their own prime contributions, arched bridges of stone and continuous paving.

The Via Appia, the *regina viarum* ("queen of roads") was begun in 312 B.C. under Appius Claudius, commissioner of public works for the year. It went south to Capua and later was extended to Brindisi, the port that served as the jump-off point for travel to the east. By the middle of the second century B.C., two trunk roads to the north had been completed, and the Italian boot was traversed its entire length by first-class highways. They were models of road engineering; Plutarch did not exaggerate by reporting that they

were carried straight across the countryside without deviation, were paved with hewn stones and bolstered underneath with masses of tight-packed sand; hollows were filled in, torrents or ravines that cut across the route were bridged, the sides were kept parallel and all on the same level—all in all, the work presented a vision of smoothness and beauty.

The paving was of polygonal blocks of hard rock such as basalt or granite; massive pieces often measuring a foot and a half across and eight inches thick, they were fitted together as cunningly as a jigsaw puzzle to form an absolutely smooth surface. They were laid on a bed, usually of packed stone or gravel and clay but also of other materials depending on the terrain. The bed was prepared with extreme care so that the blocks would stand up to any weather or traffic without sinking or erupting. The main roads were two-lane, at least eight feet wide and sometimes ten; where needed they broadened out to three lanes for stretches. Milestones all along the way let the traveler know precisely how much distance he had covered. He crossed streams on arched bridges of stone whose weight and construction guaranteed that they would not wash out.

Rome's roads and bridges involved no revolutionary technology—the Etruscans knew how to make fine roads and both they and the Greeks had used the arch—but rather bold planning, masterly organization of labor and resources, and the skill to adapt what others had done on small- to large-scale endeavors. For a revolution we must turn to Rome's buildings.

When the city of Rome was still a mere village, the Greeks were putting up impressive temples and public buildings, even theatres capable of seating thousands. Yet none of these exhibited any advances in the method of construction: this was always post and lintel, that is, based on uprights supporting horizontal beams, and the material was almost always squared stone. The Greeks' most celebrated architectural achievement, their temples, were all rectangular structures of stone blocks with pitched roofs of wooden beams and rafters covered with tiles. Their glory lay in their exquisite proportions and decoration, not their engineering. Greek theatres, which by the fourth century B.C. had grown to hold 20,000 people, were set against hillsides in order to let nature furnish the underpinning for the rising tiers of seats.

Rome's engineers had at their disposal all that the Etruscans and Greeks could teach them. Though they quickly improved on what they had learned from Etruria, it took them quite a while to emerge from under the shadow of Greek influence. When Augustus came to power he launched a program that gave the city of Rome buildings, forums, and monuments worthy of the metropolis that had become the capital of the Mediterranean world. There were some important new elements in the program, but in the main it was a continuation of what had gone on before, and Greek inspiration is unmistakable everywhere, particularly in the decoration.

Yet Roman engineers for two centuries had known a material and a building technique that were radically different and would eventually bring forth a new style of architecture destined to be among Rome's prime contributions to the western world. The material was concrete, used either by itself or with stone, and the building technique was one based on the arch and vault rather than the post and lintel. Once architects had begun to put the two new elements together to design arches and vaults of concrete, they were started on the path that was to lead to the Colosseum, the Pantheon, the Baths of Caracalla, and other celebrated structures.

In the beginning the arch or vault and concrete were used separately and only for utilitarian works. By the early second century B.C., Rome's engineers were well aware of the manifest possibilities of the arch and, in addition to arched bridges of stone, had begun to put arched gateways in walls, to erect long lines of stone arches for carrying the conduit of an aqueduct across country, and to set up that uniquely Roman form of commemorative monument, an arch standing on its own. Even earlier they had employed concrete, in a very coarse form, for foundations, walls, parts of private houses. In the second century B.C. they made their first important use of the two together when they introduced barrel vaults of concrete into their designs, as in a vast warehouse along the Tiber that was roofed with lofty barrel vaults. By the first century B.C. they had introduced the barrel vault into the construction of amphitheatres and theatres with revolutionary effect—no longer did a theatre have to lean against a hillside as in Greek cities; it could be placed anywhere its builders wanted it, with a semicircle of radially disposed barrel vaults holding up the rows of seats. At the same time they turned to another type of concrete roof, the dome; it makes its appearance in Roman architecture in the small round rooms common in bath complexes.

Vaults, domes, concrete—all had been in use in Greece and the Near East, but only for small and minor works. The Romans were the first to put them together and use them on a grand scale, thereby realizing to the full the potentialities of concrete. This was in part because they had available a superior form of it, thanks to a special type of volcanic sand that first was found near the town of Puteoli just west of Naples (we call the sand Pozzolana, after Pozzuoli, the modern name for the town) and later right around Rome. Pozzolana produced a mortar that was not only exceptionally strong but would set under water—a characteristic that opened the way to Rome's achievements in the building of bridges and harbor installations. The mix the Romans worked with was a concrete rubble, a combination of mortar with chunks of stone, rather than concrete as we know it; once set, however, it formed a monolithic mass as strong as any masonry of today.

The Roman way of erecting a wall of concrete was to build up, in a masonry of either small cut stones or bricks, the inner and outer faces of the wall to a height of a few feet; then they filled in the gap between with concrete rubble. This was repeated until the planned height was reached. Before Augustus's day, the masonry preferred for the facing had been close-set diamond-shaped stones, reticulate as it is called; during and after his reign brick became increasingly popular. Either left a pattern that was decorative enough for utilitarian works such as the barrel vaults of a warehouse, but not for the walls or ceilings of buildings of higher status. These would be stuccoed over and painted or, if money was no object, clothed in marble veneer. One of the reasons why many Roman ruins look so plain, even unsightly, is because they have lost their stucco coat or have been stripped of their marble sheath, and all that is visible is the facings enclosing the core of concrete.

In certain public buildings, such as theatres and amphitheatres, the façade was of cut stone and the guts of the structure behind it of concrete. Roman architects felt that an expanse of cut stone was not attractive enough by itself; it needed something by way of decoration. And the something they added proved so successful that it became a hallmark of western architecture, lasting until the sweeping changes of the twentieth century. They took from post and lintel architecture the column and pediment and certain other elements, which it had used structurally, and made them purely decorative. They took columns, including such allied versions as half-columns and pilasters, and pediments and disposed them so as to frame openings or to break up an expanse of a wall in aesthetically satisfying ways. The façades of the palaces and churches of Italy, of the classical-style buildings that stud Europe from Britain to Russia, of the colonial buildings of America, are in effect so many variations on this Roman theme.

Until the reign of Nero, concrete had been limited to workaday structures—warehouses, shops, apartment houses, aqueducts, the underpinnings of theatres, and so on. Under Nero it was promoted to higher uses, and the effect was revolutionary. Nero has had some bad press. His bizarre behavior during his last years has been allowed to blot out not only the decade of able and intelligent rule that preceded them but certain other claims to a better fame. He was cultivated, artistic, and possessed of a dimension shared by no other emperor, indeed by no other Greek or Roman intellectual—an avid interest in matters scientific and technological. He sent an expedition to explore the upper reaches of the Nile, devised his own pharmaceutical recipe for a stomach medicine, and had a special lens to improve his shortsighted vision. At the very moment when there were gathering about him the storm clouds of the revolt that was to end his reign, he was absorbed in perfecting an improved type of water organ. Vast building projects were a particular interest. He gave Rome the first of its great imperial baths (cf. 42 above). He undertook the herculean tasks of cutting a canal through the Isthmus of Corinth and of creating an inland waterway between Naples and Rome; though neither was brought to completion, they were feasible projects and not wild chimaeras. When the better part of Rome was wiped out by fire in A.D. 64, he personally planned the city that was to rise from the ashes, one marked by wide streets instead of the tortuous old alleys and with houses properly built of fireproof materials. At the same time, being Nero, he took over a huge portion of the burnt-out area right in the heart of town to build himself a country-style villa complex set in the midst of synthetic woodland and meadow (the Colosseum stands on what was once an artificial lake adorning it). In the villa mansion, the famous Golden House, concrete was used throughout and, in one particular room, it made possible a new and imaginative effect: the room was given an octagonal shape and this permitted it to be roofed with a dome. It is quite possible that the innovation was the brainstorm of the art-minded, technology-minded emperor himself.

Under Hadrian the potentialities of concrete were realized to the full. The monumental villa he built on the flat ground below Tivoli, some fifteen miles east of Rome, was made almost entirely of concrete and included buildings whose walls curved in and out, one part concave and the next convex; after all, with a material such as concrete, curved shapes are just as easy to make as rectilinear. These structures were

The Pantheon. Its monumental dome is the ancestor of the domes of Christian and Islamic architecture. Early second century A.D.

totally new, different, avant garde; they must have looked to Roman beholders the way world's fair architecture looks to us. The story is told that Trajan's chief architect once snapped at Hadrian, then a young fellow and offering unwanted advice, "Go draw your pumpkins!" The villa shows us what had made the old professional's gorge rise: a building there does have a melon-shaped semi-dome. Hadrian erected an avant garde building right in the middle of Rome—the Pantheon. Both Greeks and Romans had built circular temples, but always on a small scale and roofed in traditional fashion (our Jefferson Memorial in Washington gives some idea of the type and scale). Since the first century B.C., Roman architects in designing bath complexes had included small windowless round chambers topped by domes that had at their centers circular openings, oculi, or "eyes," to let in light. The Pantheon is just such a chamber, but it is freestanding like the round temples. What is new and what represents a triumph of engineering is its breathtaking scale: its dome is the biggest ever built of masonry, 142 feet in diameter, three feet wider than St. Peters's. The foundation supporting this ponderous structure is a ring of solid concrete fifteen feet deep and thirty-four broad. The wall is twenty feet thick. The dome is ingeniously constructed to diminish in weight as it leaves the wall on which it rests and rises toward the center: it grows progressively thinner, reducing to a mere five feet at the oculus, and the aggregate used in the concrete mix gets progressively lighter, going from stones of ordinary size to smaller stones to porous pumice at the oculus. The Pantheon directly inspired Brunelleschi's dome for the cathedral at Florence and Michelangelo's for St. Peters, and indirectly all the domes in western Christendom.

Another achievement of Rome's builders in concrete were the great public baths. Nero may have been the pioneer here, too, since he put up the first of them; however, little of it has survived, so we cannot be sure. In post and lintel structures, the amount of unencumbered space that can be enclosed is limited by the beams that run at regular intervals from side to side; these cannot go beyond a certain length without being supported by columns. A concrete building, on the other hand, roofed with a barrel vault or a cross vault (intersecting barrel vaults) can enclose a vast area, as in Rome's imperial bath complexes, which boast a monumental central hall covered by three soaring cross vaults. The central hall of the Baths of Diocletian was big enough to be converted by Michelangelo into a sizable church. The original Penn Station in New York City was a replica of the central hall of the Baths of Caracalla.

The Pantheon and the bath complexes and other such "modern" structures stood out in Rome the way a stark construction of steel and glass stands out in Paris or London today. For Rome's public architecture was still basically traditional. The commonest public building was the temple, and the architects of Rome's temples were conservative. So were those who designed the basilicas, the edifices that served as law courts. These were rectangular in shape, usually large and lofty, had pitched roofs, and, as support for the roof beams, had lines of columns that divided the interior into a center and side aisles—in other words, the basic features of a Christian basilica. Constantine, when deciding what the pioneer church of St. John Lateran was to be like, chose the basilica as a model, thereby establishing it as standard for Rome's Christian places of worship. Since the basilica in shape and construction was a traditional building, the architecture of the Church of Rome looked backward, as it were. Rome's "modern" style traveled with Constantine to his new capital, and with Honorius and Theodoric to Ravenna, to live on in the Byzantine churches with their curvilinear exteriors, their domes and semidomes.

For Rome's utilitarian structures, concrete continued to be the material par excellence. The apartment houses that lined her streets (cf. 37 above) were of concrete with vault-roofed shops on the ground floor. The warehouses that lined the Tiber were of concrete. The aqueducts that the emperors added to enable the water supply to keep up with the ever growing population marched across the open country on concrete arches. The Colosseum consists of a skeleton of cut stone fleshed out with concrete. Rome's concrete, able to set under water, made possible the mighty new harbor that was built just north of Ostia (73 above).

We know about the Roman art of building not only from the ruins that have survived but also from a textbook that has survived—M. Vitruvius Pollio's *On Architecture.*

Vitruvius trained himself specifically for the profession of architect. He seems to have started his career in the army; at one time he was in charge of maintenance and development of engines of war. He served both Caesar and Augustus, particularly the latter, and in his old age wrote the work that made him famous, dedicating it to Augustus. It has ten divisions, or books as they are called: Book One takes up the qualifications of an architect, the nature of architecture, town sites, town planning; Two takes up materials; Three and Four, temples; Five, public buildings; Six, private houses; Seven, interior decoration; Eight, water, its sources and properties, its uses for leveling, how to pipe it in, and so on; Nine, sundials and other means for measuring time; Ten, engines of war and construction machinery. What use Augustus may have made of it, we don't know. What we do know is that it became a veritable bible for architects of the Renaissance and through them affected generations of followers.

The work is far from a bald handbook of building techniques. To Vitruvius a good architect was not a narrow professional but an intellectual of wide-ranging abilities, "a man of letters, a skillful draughtsman, instructed in geometry, versed in history, and a diligent student of philosophy; he should understand music, have some knowledge of medicine, know the opinions of jurists, and be acquainted with astronomy." He must be a man of letters to write up his knowledge; a draughtsman so that he can draw up his own sketches of his work. He must: know geometry since "it teaches us the use of the rule and the compass, and this facilitates the planning of buildings on their sites, and the truing of these by the use of the square, level, and plumb bob"; be versed in history because "he should be able to explain to enquirers the rationale behind many of the ornaments often included in an architect's design"; know philosophy since it "makes an architect highminded . . . and free of greed, which is all-important for no work can be accomplished without good faith and honesty"; understand music in order to be able to "tune" the tension of the cords that propel catapults; have some knowledge of medicine in order to answer questions "of air, the healthiness and unhealthiness of sites, the water supply, for without such considerations no habitation can be regarded as healthy"; know the opinions of jurists in order to draw up specifications that will conform with regulations and property rights; and he must be acquainted with astronomy in order to set up sundials in the proper way.

Vitruvius's conception of architecture is no less wide, at times almost approaching what we define as urban studies. Take his pronouncements on the choice of a site for a city. The very first consideration must be salubrity: one must avoid marshy land, places that are troubled by cloud or frost, places that are mercilessly exposed to the sun. Once an appropriate site has been picked, one must keep very carefully in mind the direction of the prevailing winds in orienting the streets. Winds must not blow directly upon a street, for the effect is uniformly bad: "if they are cold, they injure, if hot infect, if humid harm." In discussing public buildings he warns that a theatre should not be put near marshy areas since the spectators, who consist of whole families, men and women and children, spend long hours seated without moving and will thus undergo extended exposure to the unhealthy marsh winds. Nor should it be oriented toward the south, for then the air, which in a theatre has little chance to circulate, will get excessively hot and be damaging to the body. Bath complexes must be in the warmest possible site, sheltered on the north and northeast. The hot rooms should be lighted from the west, or from the south if the site rules out the west, since the usual time for people to come to the baths is between midday and evening rather than during the morning hours. In dealing with private houses, he reminds the architect to take cognizance of climate: in the north houses should be all closed in and face the direction that offers the most warmth; in the south they should be open to the air and have a northern or northeastern exposure.

Vitruvius wrote almost one hundred years before the architectural revolution that began in Nero's reign. The architecture he describes is largely traditional, the style in which his patron was rebuilding the capital. In this area he provides us with a precious store of information, from the proportions to be used in planning public buildings to the techniques of painting and stuccoing, from the dimensions of marble columns to those of lead pipes, from the design of derricks to the design of waterclocks—a detailed exposition, in sum, of one of the areas in which Rome's genius shone most brightly.

Underneath many of Europe's present highways are the roads that were part of Rome's great network. The Roman way of decorating a building set a pattern that lasted until this century. The Pantheon, the Baths of Caracalla and Deocletian, Vitruvius's descriptions and pronouncements, all inspired architects from Michelangelo to the designers of railroad terminals. Our debt to Rome's engineers is tangible and ubiquitous.

CHAPTER XIII

The Emperor

When Hadrian succeeded to the rulership of Rome in A.D. 117, the empire had been in being for nearly a century and a half. With superb statesmanship, a profound understanding of precisely what the empire needed, and total dedication to the task of being its ruler, Hadrian took the machinery of government that Augustus had fashioned, by then creaking in many parts, repaired it to fit changed times and new needs, and thereby gave it centuries more of life. Everywhere we turn we see the touch of his hand: in the dispositions of legions on the farthest frontiers, in a codification of the law at Rome, in a revamped imperial bureaucracy, in the thousands of monuments whose remains spangle Europe or the thousands of sculptures that he commissioned and which now fill its museums. The Roman Empire was the longest-lived in history; Augustus created it, but he must share with Hadrian the credit for its longevity.

Hadrian was of Spanish extraction, as was his cousin Trajan, who, being childless, selected him and trained him to be heir to the throne. Spain and France, North Africa, Asia Minor, and other well-developed provinces, were no longer appanages of Italy; they were the parts of which the empire was the sum. It took rulers with roots in Spain to recognize this and adjust policy accordingly. Trajan devoted much care to the administration of the provinces; however, a born soldier, he was happier in a tent than an office and spent a good part of his reign waging war, first in pacifying and annexing what is today Rumania and then in a campaign to conquer Rome's troublesome eastern neighbors, a bloody three years that brought precious little to show for the cost in men and money.

Hadrian, though Trajan's equal as a soldier, chose to be a statesman. He pulled the army out of the East, cut Rome's losses, and concentrated on maintaining peace—which, he was perfectly aware, meant being as military-minded as Trajan had been: "He desired peace rather than war, yet he trained his troops as if war were imminent," is the way an ancient biographer put it. He gave the army meticulous attention, updating its regulations, allowing the legions to recruit locally and thereby avoid time-consuming shifting of men, insisting on constant and strenuous maneuvers. These he supervised personally whenever he could. We have the text of a speech he delivered on one such occasion in A.D. 128 at the fort of Lambaesis in Algeria—it was carved on stone there—and the emperor's words reveal that he had the details of everything that went on at his fingertips. When inspecting units, he lived the ordinary legionary's life, sleeping in the open air, eating army chow, doing a day's march with full pack. He overhauled the fortifications along the frontier, strengthening the bulwarks that existed and building new ones where needed. The wall he raised in Britain still stands, a mighty rampart that runs seventy-four miles clean across the waist of the island from the Tyne to the Solway; it protected the Romanized province of Britain from attacks at the hands of savage Scottish tribes. Nothing, however, is without its price. The maintenance of an army primarily for defense, with the troops passing much of their lives around their local base, imperceptibly weakened morale by engendering a defensive mentality and military laxness, particularly under emperors who did not exert themselves as Hadrian did to make the soldiers toe the mark. And recruiting legions from local populations was the first step toward barbarizing the army, leading to the time when Rome would have only non-Romans to count on for protection. All this, however, lay far

ahead, beyond any human foresight; Hadrian's well-conceived arrangements gave the empire peace and security for half a century.

Of Hadrian's two decades on the throne, one was spent in ceaseless
travel about the empire. When Trajan died in southern Asia Minor, en
route home from the futile campaign in the East, Hadrian was in Syria.
He was not able to get back to Rome until the spring of A.D. 118.
Within two years he had settled matters there sufficiently to embark
on his first journey, from which he was not to return for six years.
He started with a swing through the West: France, Germany, Britain,
Spain, and the part of North Africa opposite Spain. In 123 he left Spain
to sail directly to Ephesus in Asia Minor for a tour of the eastern part of
his realm. He traveled the length and breadth of Asia Minor, passed by
boat through the Aegean islands to visit Athens and make a circuit of
Greece, and finally reappeared in Rome toward the end of 126. But the
capital did not hold its restless ruler very long. After about a year he was
off again, first for a trip to what is today Tunisia and Algeria and back,
and then for another long swing through the East. After revisiting
Greece and Asia Minor, he pushed on to Syria, Arabia, and Egypt. This
is when he went up the Nile with his entourage to visit Memnon, and
the statue was ungracious enough not to talk for him. By 131 he was
back in Rome to stay.

Hadrian's travels were not junkets for play and sightseeing, although
he indulged in a good deal of both for relaxation. Wherever he went he
made inquiries, listened attentively, took careful thought, and issued
commands. The results ran the gamut from revamping the farm legislation for a large part of North Africa to putting up a new monument
over the tomb of Alcibiades. His trail is blazed with an unending series
of public works, fortifications for the frontiers, and monuments, temples, buildings, roads, aqueducts, and what not for everywhere else. In
Britain he ordered the famous wall, in France a new temple at Nîmes,
in Spain repairs to a temple of Augustus at Tarragona and a set of new
roads. In the East he founded several towns, most of them not surprisingly named Hadrianopolis, rebuilt others that had been destroyed by
earthquake, put up a temple at Cyzicus that became one of the "marvels

of the world," and had the governor of a province on the Black Sea draw up a report on that body of water, one of the few works of its kind that has survived. In Greece he was particularly lavish. One town got a new temple, another a colonnade, Corinth a set of baths and an aqueduct, Eleusis—where he was initiated into the mysteries—a bridge. The prizes were reserved for Athens: he built a whole new quarter there, whose entrance arch still stands, put up an enormous quadrilateral colonnade with a library attached to it, and completed a gargantuan temple to Zeus that had been left unfinished for three centuries.

The last years of Hadrian's life, from 131 to 138, were spent at Rome, with one exception: in 132 and 133 he was in the East watching from closer at hand the army operations involved in putting down a bitter revolt of the Jews. Hadrian was one of Rome's greatest rulers, but even a great ruler can make mistakes, particularly when dealing with a minority group whose ways are strange and beyond his experience. Jews under Rome's administration suffered the difficulties that Christians were soon to meet for the same reason: the exclusiveness of their god made them a people apart in a pagan world, where state and religion were inextricably bound together. Neither Jews nor Christians could hail a Roman emperor as a living god, an act that was almost second nature to the inhabitants of the eastern empire, nor worship the spirits of deified dead emperors, which was an officially maintained cult. Hadrian decided to settle the Jewish problem once and for all: he ordered a new pagan city to be built over the site of Jerusalem with a temple to Zeus on the spot where Solomon's had stood, and he banned circumcision. The inevitable result was the fanatically desperate Bar Kochba revolt, which ended only with the extermination of the rebels. Archaeologists have recently brought to light pathetic evidence of the last survivors; families had fled to remote caves for refuge and, unable to leave since the enemy was all about, starved to death there, men, women, and children. It was three years before Hadrian could again turn his mind to the works of peace, where his true genius lay.

The very years of the revolt saw the launching of one of the monumental acts of his reign: a codification of Roman law, carried out by

Salvius Julianus. He thereby not only changed the basic nature of the law—its source was now the emperor and no longer Rome's judicial officials—but laid the foundation for the magisterial development that was summed up in Justinian's famous codification and through it became the law of most of Western Europe.

One other great change that Hadrian introduced was in the staffing of the administration. When Augustus founded the empire, he had followed the standard practice of using slaves and freedmen for handling the government's growing bookkeeping (cf. 58, 60 above). This eventually led to a topsy-turvy situation in which some of the most powerful state offices were in the hands of ex-slaves, who were able to use their positions to become among the richest and most influential personages in the realm. That these men were the best fitted for the job was beside the point; they were a constant source of irritation, and in the reigns of Claudius and Nero, when their power was at its height, they laid the emperor open to bitter criticism. Hadrian turned over most of the significant offices previously held by freedmen to members of the class of gentry just below the senators, assigning them appropriate titles and salaries. The result was the creation of a formal imperial bureaucracy. Suetonius, for example, held an important clerkship—one of Pliny's friends had gotten it for him—until Hadrian fired him for not treating the empress with respect.

And Hadrian gets the credit for yet another precedent-setting move—the return of the beard. He let his grow, thereby ending more than five clean-shaven centuries and launching two bearded ones; it was Constantine who reversed the fashion and once again drove Roman gentlemen to the daily session at the barbershop.

Religion was an important part of the apparatus of government, and Hadrian gave it scrupulous attention. His two biggest building projects at Rome were temples, the Temple of Venus and Rome and the Pantheon. He even erected a temple to the divinity of his mother-in-law, about the handsomest gesture any son-in-law has ever made. He took his duties as Pontifex Maximus, titular head of the official Roman cult, with utmost seriousness. He was equally concerned with the religions of the provinces: he restored old sanctuaries, revived old festivals, such as those in honor of Dionysus at Athens, respectfully consulted the Delphic oracle. He had the weakness of his age for astrology; an ancient biographer gravely assures us that he foresaw the day of his own death. By far the most puzzling aspect of Hadrian's attitude toward religion, however, concerns the boy whose face is one of the best known from the ancient world—Antinoüs.

He was a native of a small town in Bithynia, a province on the south shore of the Black Sea. Hadrian met him when traveling through the area, probably in A.D. 124, during his first journey. The boy, spectacularly good-looking, became the emperor's favorite page. Hadrian got scant satisfaction from his wife, whom he had married for political reasons and who had turned out to be vain and petulant; she let it be known that she had no intention of ever giving him a child. Moreover, like so many of his contemporaries, he enjoyed homosexual as well as heterosexual relations. Antinoüs was with the entourage when it sailed up the Nile to visit Memnon in 130 and somehow was drowned. Was it an accident? Or a well-maneuvered shove by someone who thought the scandal had to be brought to an end? Or suicide, as some said—Antinoüs, no less superstitious than the next man, sacrificing his own life to forestall a death predicted for the emperor? We do not know. What we do know is that Hadrian went wild with grief and set about commemorating his favorite with monuments worthy of an emperor, even raising him to the ranks of the immortals. He founded a city, Antinoöpolis, near the spot where the drowning occurred. At Mantinea in Greece, which according to tradition had sent out a thousand years earlier the immigrants who founded the boy's birthplace, he built a temple for Antinoüs's worship; there was another at Lanuvium, just twenty miles from Rome, and a humble social club there claimed Antinoüs as one of its protectors along with Diana (43 above). A mystery cult based on his divinity was founded at Mantinea, as well as a quadrennial festival in his honor. Similar festivals were celebrated at Athens, Eleusis, Argos; they were still being held two hundred years later. Even an oracle was established, where priests issued prophecies in

Hadrian. British Museum, London.

the new god's name. Everywhere statues of him went up—Antinoüs as Hermes, Antinoüs as Apollo, as Osiris, as Ganymede. No less than five hundred sculptures of him have survived, twice the number of Hadrian's; the almost too perfect sensual features are on display in dozens of museums. Hadrian willed him to be a god, and the world of the second century accepted him along with all its other deities.

Hadrian the statesman, soldier, legalist, administrator—all these form but one side of this complex human being. There is also the man who exchanged ripostes with the intellectual luminaries of the age, spent a fortune on a pleasure villa, divinized a mortal—even with a wealth of biographical data we would find it hard to comprehend him, and as it is, all we have is a skimpy account drawn up by some hack at least a century and a half after its subject's death. When it comes to dealing with Hadrian's multifaceted interests, skills, and personality, the author is reduced to spluttering antitheses:

He was an ardent student of poetry and letters, and extremely well versed in mathematics, geometry, painting. He openly vaunted his skill in singing and playing the lyre. In sensual pleasures he went to excess, even composing many a poem about the objects of his passion. Yet he was expert with weapons, profoundly knowledgeable in military affairs, and also knew how to handle gladiator's arms. He was stern yet gay, affable yet serious, careless yet cautious, grasping yet generous, dissembling yet open-faced, cruel yet merciful—forever changeable in everything.

Hadrian has puzzled far more sophisticated brains than his simple-minded biographer's. The man who codified Rome's laws and founded its bureaucracy was at the same time a trained athlete, an excellent horseman with a passion for hunting who not only gleefully slew beasts himself but arranged to have thousands slaughtered in the gladiatorial games he sponsored. The man who fostered the first legislation guaranteeing some degree of humanity in the treatment of slaves sold off so many captives after the Jewish war that the market was glutted and the site in Gaza where the auctions took place was for centuries afterward known as Hadrian's Market. The man who knew how to handle gladiatorial arms was equally at home with the sculptor's chisel, artist's brush, and architect's compass and rule. Whatever pictures or statues he turned out have been lost, but the results of his ventures in architecture still stand. At Tivoli he built the villa to end all villas: spread over some 180 acres, with a seven-mile circumference, it boasted two theatres, three sets of baths, libraries, endless porticoes—a veritable city with the room and facilities to accommodate thousands. The décor included not only mosaics and murals but statues by the hundreds, chiefly replicas of renowned Greek masterpieces. The site was honeycombed with underground passageways so that the army of hard-working slaves who provided the services stayed discreetly out of view.

The numerous works that Hadrian fostered throughout the empire were all in traditional style and are remarkable more for grandeur, at times grandioseness, than daring innovation. In Rome he was responsible for at least two important structures besides the Pantheon. One was the huge temple to Venus and Rome that faces the Colosseum; the other was his tomb. It too was traditional in design, being a more elaborate version of Augustus's, a gigantic drumlike mound sheathed in marble. By the sixth century A.D. it had begun its conversion from mausoleum to fortress, and in the ensuing centuries it was refashioned to become the impregnable Castel Sant' Angelo.

If time has spared us some of the products of Hadrian the architect, it has been far less generous with Hadrian the man of letters. The emperor spent long hours amid a coterie of intellectuals of all kinds, particularly the literary lights of the day. As with art, he was not only connoisseur but practitioner, in both prose and verse. We know that he produced an autobiography, but neither it nor any other of his prose works has survived. His biographers quote some of his verse, and if their samples are any indication, Hadrian was poetaster rather than poet. When a friend named Florus sent him this trifle,

Caesar would I never be,
tramping round through Brittany.

hiding out in Germany
bitten by cold in Hungary,

the emperor responded,

Make me not a Florus, please!
tramping round through beaneries,
hiding out in eateries,
bitten by the big fat fleas.

Then, at the very end of his life, the vision through death's door inspired him to a minor masterpiece.

Disease is no respecter even of an athlete's body. Hadrian, as he neared his sixties, retired to his villa, but that architectural fairyland, where he no doubt had planned to spend his last years in calm serenity, was the scene of agony. Sickness struck him, and the pain got so intense that he begged a servant, an ex-huntsman, to end it with a dagger and tried to get his doctor to administer poison; a Roman emperor was not allowed the exit of suicide. He grimly carried on the business of state, as clear-headed as ever, and on the last birthday he was to see, January 24, 138, since his wife had made good on her threat and he had no children, he submitted to the Senate the name of his chosen successor, Antoninus Pius. When the heat of summer turned even the chambers of his villa to an inferno, he gathered what scant strength he had left and set off for Baiae. There, on the point of death, he wrote the little poem that has become deservedly famous. It is done in the mocking tone of his light verse, but it mocks no light subject:

Animula vagula, blandula,
hospes comesque corporis,
quae nunc abibis in loca
pallidula, rigida, nudula?
Nec ut soles dabis jocos.

Sweet soulkin, flitting, fair,
my body's guest and friend,

I wonder where you'll end.
a ghostlet, stiffened, bare?
You'll miss your jesting there.

Epilogue

When Hadrian died, things were running so smoothly that the new emperor never once had to leave Italy during his two decades of rule. No disturbance troubled the peace and calm of the land. Antoninus Pius, too, had no children. He confirmed as his successor the man Hadrian had provisionally designated twenty-three years earlier. The choice reveals the keen judgment of both: it was Marcus Aurelius, the philosopher-emperor, who replaced him on the throne.

Then the storm broke—trouble on the eastern borders, a devastating plague brought back from there by the troops, and worst of all, barbarian invasions. Behind the fortifications that Hadrian had so carefully laid out, thousands of tribesmen were seething with unrest under pressures that originated as far away as Mongolia; they spilled over the frontiers, inundating farmland and city. Like Hadrian, Aurelius spent most of his reign far away from Rome; unlike him, his days were devoted to the work of war, not peace, doggedly throwing back the intruders. And unlike all three who preceded him, he had a son, Commodus, whom he carefully trained for the succession. The philosopher-king, whose reign was devoted to selfless performance of harsh duty, had no inkling that he was turning the empire over to someone whose reign would be devoted to selfish satisfaction of vicious tastes. In due time there was the inevitable assassination, then the nadir, when the throne was auctioned off. Eventually an able soldier came to the fore, Septimius Severus, who set the empire on its feet and marched the armies to even greater victories than Trajan's.

On his deathbed the advice he gave his two sons was, "Stick together, pay the soldiers plenty, and forget about everything else." The lifestyle that had begun with Augustus and reached its apogee under Hadrian was a thing of the past.

The Roman Emperors of the First and Second Centuries

Augustus	27 B.C.–A.D. 14	Domitian	81–96
Tiberius	A.D. 14–37	Nerva	96–98
Gaius (Caligula)	37–41	Trajan	98–117
Claudius	41–54	Hadrian	117–138
Nero	54–68	Antoninus Pius	138–161
Galba	68–69	Marcus Aurelius	161–180
Otho	69	Commodus	176–192
Vitellius	69	Pertinax	193
Vespasian	69–79	Didius Julianus	193
Titus	79–81	Severus	193–211

Abbreviations

Balsdon	J. Balsdon, *Life and Leisure in Ancient Rome* (London 1969).
Carcopino	J. Carcopino, *Daily Life in Ancient Rome*, trans. E. Lorimer (London 1941).
Casson	L. Casson, *Travel in the Ancient World*[2] (Baltimore 1994).
Casson, *AM*	L. Casson, *The Ancient Mariners*[2] (Princeton 1991).
CIL	*Corpus Inscriptionum Latinarum.*
Crook	J. Crook, *Law and Life of Rome* (Ithaca, N.Y. 1967).
Dill	S. Dill, *Roman Society from Nero to Marcus Aurelius*[2] (London 1905).
ESAR	T. Frank, ed., *An Economic Survey of Ancient Rome* (Baltimore 1933–1940).
Finley	M. Finley, *The Ancient Economy*[2] (Berkeley 1985).
Grant	M. Grant, *The World of Rome* (NAL 1960).
Henderson	B. Henderson, *The Life and Principate of the Emperor Hadrian* (London 1923).

Homo   L. Homo, *Rome impériale et l'urbanisme dans l'antiquité*[2] (Paris 1971).

IGRR   R. Cagnat, ed., *Inscriptiones Graecae ad res Romanas pertinentes* (Paris 1901–1927).

ILS   H. Dessau, *Inscriptiones Latinae selectae* (Berlin 1892–1916).

JRS   Journal of Roman Studies.

Lewis-Reinhold   N. Lewis and M. Reinhold, *Roman Civilization, Sourcebook II: The Empire*[3] (New York 1990).

Mau-Kelsey   A. Mau, *Pompeii: Its Life and Art*, trans. F. Kelsey (New York 1899).

Meiggs   R. Meiggs, *Roman Ostia*[2] (Oxford 1973).

Sel. Pap.   A. Hunt and C. Edgar, *Select Papyri* (Loeb Classical Library 1932–1934).

Starr   C. Starr, *The Roman Imperial Navy*[2] (Cambridge 1960).

Syll.   W. Dittenberger, *Sylloge inscriptionum Graecarum*[3] (Leipzig 1915–1924).

Tarn-Griffith   W. Tarn and G. Griffith, *Hellenistic Civilisation*[3] (London 1952).

Ward-Perkins   A. Boëthius and J. Ward-Perkins, *Etruscan and Roman Architecture* (Penguin 1970).

Watson   G. Watson, *The Roman Soldier* (Ithaca, N.Y. 1969).

White   K. White, *Roman Farming* (Ithaca, N.Y. 1970).

Notes

Chapter I. The Times

6   "sheep sheared": Dio Cassius 57.10.5.

6–8   Extension of citizenship: Crook 41–42. "put every Greek": *Apocolocynthesis divi Claudii* 3.3. Tarsus's citizenship status: Cf. C. Welles in *Mélanges Université St. Joseph* 38.2 (1962) 59–62. Rome's population: *ESAR* v, 218; L. Casson in *Memoirs of the American Academy in Rome* 36 (1980) 23.

Chapter II. The Family

10–13   *paterfamilias*: Crook 107–110. Marriage, dowry: Crook 99–105. Betrothal: W. Becker, trans. by F. Metcalfe, *Gallus* (London 1903) 170–171. Ring: Carcopino 80–81. Marriage ceremony: Becker 159–167. "The contract's signed": Juvenal 2.119–120. *Ubi tu Gaius:* Plutarch, *Mor.* 271e. Divorce: Crook 105–106; Becker 175–176. *Tua res tibi*: E. Warmington, *Remains of Old Latin* (Loeb Classical Library 1938) iii, p. 442. Cicero's troubles: Cicero, *Att.* 16.15.5–6 (Terentia); *Att.* 12.8, *Fam.* 6.18.5 (Tullia). Number of slaves: Balsdon 197.

14–15   Childlessness, contraception, abortion: K. Hopkins in *Comparative Studies in Society and History* 8 (1965/1966) 124–151; Balsdon 82–86. "liver of a cat": Aëtius 16.17. "Gemellus": Martial 1.10. Historical figures as foundlings: Balsdon 87. "from the dump": R. Taubenschlag, *The Law of Greco-Roman Egypt*[2] (Warsaw 1955) 74.

16   Assistance programs: Lewis-Reinhold 255–259. "of one million sesterces": *CIL* 10.6328 (cf. Lewis-Reinhold 268). Constantine allows sale of children: Balsdon 88.

16–17   Birth ceremonies: Balsdon 90. Boy's coming of age ceremony: Becker (op. cit. under 10–13) 195–196. Children's games: Balsdon 91. School: Balsdon 92–99; Becker 187–195.

17–21   Slaves: Balsdon 106–115; cf. Chapter 6 above. Difficulty of learning Latin: Balsdon 107. Bedding, no wearing of hose: Carcopino 152–153. Marketing done by the masters: Carcopino 183. Meals and dining: Carcopino 263–266. Dinners ready cooked, snack bars: Casson 211, 213. Courses: Balsdon 41–42. Graces, Muses: Aulus Gellius 13.11.2. Exotic foods, Caesar's banquet: Balsdon 43–44. Chill with snow: Carcopino 269. Costs: Balsdon 37. Juvenal's ignominy: Juvenal 5.24–155. Entertainment: Balsdon 46–49. Family festivals: Balsdon 122–125.

21–23   Undertakers: Becker (op. cit. under 10–13) 507. "Let's admit it": Juvenal 3.171–172. Funerals: Becker 511–515. Tombs: Crook 133–138. "From this tomb": *ILS* 8365. Paupers' graves: Meiggs 463–464. "To the spirits of the departed": *ILS* 7674 (cf. Lewis-Reinhold 197).

Chapter III. On the Farm

24–26   "As usual": Pliny 3.19. Gentleman's investment: Finley 121–122. Accumulation of land: Finley 101–104. Tunisia's six owners: *ESAR* v, 43. Huge farm in France: Finley 112. Livestock in southern Italy: *ESAR* v, 163. Grain in Po Valley, Campania: *ESAR* v, 145. Wine country: *ESAR* v, 146–147. Olives: *ESAR* v, 155. Vines favored: *ESAR* v, 141–142. Olives sold locally: *ESAR* v, 153, 156.

26–28   Difficulties with tenants: White 406–408. Sharecropping: Pliny 9.37. Slave-run farms: White 350–352. Treatment of slaves: Columella 1.8 (cf. Lewis-Reinhold 89). Cato's advice: White 358. *vilicus*: White 353–354. Agent: White 353. "whether the slaves": Columella 1.8.16–18. Hired labor: White 347–350. Dangerous jobs: Varro, *de Re Rustica* 1.17.2. "merely increased": R. Cotterill, *The Old South* (Glendale 1936) 263. Few resident landlords: W. Heitland, *Agricola* (Cambridge 1921) 224.

28–29   Dry farming: G. Steiner in C. Roebuck, ed., *The Muses at Work* (Cambridge, Mass. 1969) 162–165. Vegetables: *ESAR* v, 159–160. Fruits, nuts: D. Casella in *Raccolta di studi per il secondo centenario degli scavi di Pompei* (Naples 1950) 360–386. The barnyard: Steiner 159; *ESAR* v, 168. Livestock, work animals: White, Chap. 10. Bees: *ESAR* v, 168.

29   Farm equipment: White 448–450. Wheelbarrow: Cf. J. Needham, *Science and Civilisation in China* iv.2 (Cambridge 1965) 258–274. Water mill: White 446–447; L. White, *Medieval Technology and Social Change* (Oxford 1962) 79–83.

Chapter IV. In the City

30   "I found Rome": Suetonius, *Aug.* 28.3. Residential quarters: Homo 478–482.

31–33   Telling time: Balsdon 17–19. Bedchamber, sleeping in underclothes: Carcopino 152–153. Toga: Carcopino 154–155. Wife's bedchamber: Carcopino 165. Martial's cutting lines: Carcopino 11.104.7–8. Women's dress, make-up: Carcopino 166–170. Furnishings: Carcopino 152–153 (bedroom), 33–35 (sitting room), 35–38 (heating, lighting).

33–34   Morning call, working day: Balsdon 21–26. Barber: Carcopino 157–164. Dinner suit: Balsdon 34. Dark clothing: The Latin term for "common people" was *pullati,* "the dark ones." Lights on Pompeian stores: Casson 262.

34–35   No day of rest: Balsdon 64. Roman calendar, craftsmen's holidays, apprenticeship contracts: Balsdon 75–77.

35–37   Brutus's loan: *ESAR* i, 388–389. Crassus: Plutarch, *Crassus* 2.3–4. Narcissus, Pallas: *ESAR* v, 57. Their houses: Homo 478–479. "a cargo of wine": Petronius 76. "He wants an art": Martial 5.56. Teachers: Carcopino 104–105. Doctors: Balsdon 132–133. Lawyers paid in kind: Martial 12.72. "Not poison, murder": Martial 6.19.

37–38   Rome a city of apartment houses: Homo 477. Apartments scarce and expensive: Homo 524–532. Renting of dark holes: Homo 507–508. Fires and collapse: Homo 512–514, 526–528. "two of my shops": Cicero, *Att.* 14.9.1.

38–40   Aqueducts: R. Lanciani, *The Ruins and Excavations of Ancient Rome* (Boston 1897) 47–58; Homo 186–198. Fountains: Homo 180. Illegal pipes: Homo 190. Grain supply: *ESAR* v, 218–220; Homo 205–210. Sewers: Lanciani 28–31; Homo 244–245, 304. Latrines: Homo 304–305; Carcopino 41. Street-cleaning: Homo 420–422. "Think . . . of the number": Juvenal 3.270–277. Rome's law on dumping: Homo 559–566. "Against those who pour": *Dig.* 9.3. Police: Homo 148–152, 156–157. Fire department: Homo 163–184.

42–44   Baths: Balsdon 26–32. "What worse than Nero": Martial 7.34.4–5. Porticos, gardens: Homo 399–414. Libraries: Homo 261–264; Balsdon 148–149. Museums: Casson 246–251. Clubs: Dill 144–137. "It was voted": *ILS* 7212 (cf. Lewis-Reinhold 186–188). Trade association headquarters at Ostia: Meiggs 324–325.

44–46   Narrow streets: Homo 370–372. Caesar's law: Homo 433–434; Carcopino 49–50. "I hurry": Juvenal 3.243–248. Shopkeepers spill into streets: Homo 431–432. Noise: Carcopino 48–50. Lubricants: Casson 179. "It takes a lot": Juvenal 3.235. "Here is the prelude": Juvenal 3.288–301. Street lighting: Homo 581–584; Casson 262–263.

46–47 Street names: Homo 377–384. House numbers: Homo 588–589. "You know that house": Terence, *Adelphoe* 581–584. "He told me": Plautus, *Pseudolus* 596–597. Letters: Casson 221. "Return me to the house": *CIL* 15.7190.

Chapter V. A Roman Gentleman

48 Helped ladies: Pliny 2.4, 3.3. Recommendations for children: 4.15. Health of his staff: 5.19.

49–50 Uncle's death: Pliny 6.16. Wrote a tragedy: 7.4.2. Studied under Quintilian: 6.6.3. Army service: 1.10.1, 3.11.5, 7.31.2. Political career: 7.16.2, 3.18.1. Commissioner of sewers: *ILS* 2927.5. Five-hour speech: Pliny 2.11.14.

50 Letter to wife's aunt: Pliny 4.19.3–4. Wife's miscarriage: 8.10.

51–52 House on the Esquiline: Pliny 3.21.5. "If you ask someone": 1.9.2. Spent three days listening: 4.27.1. Three days reading: 3.18.4. Behavior at recitations: 1.13.2, 6.17. Collaboration with Tacitus: 2.11.2. Favors for Suetonius: 10.94–95. Gift to Martial: 3.21.2. "You know me": 9.23.2–3.

52–54 Seaside villa: Pliny 2.17. Near Ostia, equipped with baths: 2.17.2, 26. "I wake when I please": 9.36. Fish from window: 9.7.4. "I have no slaves": 3.19.7. Tenant trouble: 9.37. Rebates on grape crop: 8.2.

54–55 "Do you go to school": Pliny 4.13. Request of recommendations from Tacitus: 4.13.10–11. Endowment for needy children: 7.18. Baths, library, endowments for freedmen: *ILS* 2927.9–14 (cf. Lewis-Reinhold 269–270). Temple: Pliny 4.1.5. Shrine: 9.39.

55–56 Faulty aqueduct: Pliny 10.37. Canal: 10.41. Fire department: 10.33. Nicaea: 10.39.1–4. Claudiopolis: 10.39.5. Amastris: 10.98. Sinope: 10.90. "The sum and substance": 10.96.7–8. Wife's journey: 10.120.

Chapter VI. The Slave

57 "I was no bigger": Petronius 75–76.

58–60 Limited slavery in ancient Near East: M. Finley in *Comparative Studies in Society and History* 6 (1963 / 1964) 238. Greco-Roman slavery: Finley

70–71, 78–79. White-collar work done by slaves: Finley 73, 75–76; Crook 187. Slave banker: T. Glover, *From Pericles to Philip*[2] (London 1918) 312–313 (career of Pasion); cf. *ESAR* v, 28. Slave crews: L. Casson, *Ships and Seamanship in the Ancient World*[3] (Baltimore 1995) 328. Slave real-estate agents: Homo 522. Athens's navy clerks: B. Jordan, *The Athenian Navy in the Classical Period* (Berkeley 1975) 60. Galley rowers: Casson *AM*, 87.

60–61   Roman manumission: Finley in *Comparative Studies* (op cit. under 58–60) 243. Imperial civil service: Crook 62–63. Manumission at thirty to thirty-five: P. Weaver, *Familia Caesaris* (Cambridge 1972) 104. Pallas, Narcissus: Weaver 263. "Once when Claudius": Suetonius, *Claudius* 28. Felix: Weaver 282. Commanders of fleets: Starr 32.

61–62   Musicus Scurranus: *ILS* 1514 (cf. G. de Ste Croix, *The Class Struggle in the Ancient Greek World* [Ithaca 1981] 143); Weaver (op cit. under 60–61) 201. Julian's barber: Ammianus Marcellinus 22.4.9. Slaves as masters' partners: Crook 189. Free man sells himself: Crook 59–60. "My father": Petronius 57.

62   Women's employment: S. Treggiari in *American Journal of Ancient History* 1 (1976) 78–96. "My god": Cicero, *Fam.* 9.26.2. Cytheris and Mark Antony: Plutarch, *Antony* 9.4. Acte: Suetonius, *Nero* 28.1, 50. Vespasian's concubine (Caenis): Suetonius, *Vespasian* 3.

62–63   Ex-slaves as high proportion of citizenry, as a middle class: Crook 50. Freedmen at heart of society in Ostia: Meiggs 217. Eutychus: Meiggs 181–182. "from the interest on which": Meiggs 561, no. 14.8–11. Eutychus's son: Meiggs 211. "as a coopted member": Meiggs 561, no. 14.1–7.

63–64   Upward mobility of ex-slaves: M. Gordon in *JRS* 21 (1931) 65–77. Purchase of honors, favored banquets and gladiatorial games: Gordon 74–75. Horace's father: Horace, *Sat.* 1.6.62–88. "a monument": Horace, *Odes* 3.30.

Chapter VII. Two Resurrected Cities

65–66   "For several days": Pliny 6.20.3–18.

66   William Hamilton: E. Corti, *The Destruction and Resurrection of Pompeii and Herculaneum*, trans. by K. and R. Smith (London 1951) 137–138. Excavations: Mau-Kelsey 25–29.

67–69   Pompeii's history: Mau-Kelsey 8–18. Development of Pompeian house: Mau-Kelsey 239–268, esp. 239–240. Villas: E. La Rocca, M. and

A. deVos, *Pompei²* (Milan 1994) 350–360. Villa of the Mysteries: La Rocca-deVos 354–360. House of the Vettii: L. Richardson, *Pompeii: An Architectural History* (Baltimore 1988) 324–329, esp. 324. Old houses altered for commercial use: Richardson 20–21. House of Sallust altered: Mau-Kelsey 281. Population: *ESAR* v, 252. Murals: Mau-Kelsey 446–460. Mosaics: Mau-Kelsey 272; cf. 282, 287–288 (House of the Faun). Statuary: Mau-Kelsey 438–441.

69–70   Baths: A. and M. deVos, *Pompei, Ercolano, Stabia* (Bari 1982) 49–52 (Terme del Foro), 58 (Terme del Sarno), 194–202 (Terme Stabiane). Amphitheatre: Mau-Kelsey 206–220. Theatres: Mau-Kelsey 135–150. Forum buildings: Mau-Kelsey 44–45, Plan ii. Pompeii's officials: Mau-Kelsey 12–14.

70–71   Taverns: Casson 211–216. "Add cold water": *CIL* 4.1291. "I'm out": *CIL* 4.3494. Brothels: deVos (op. cit. under 67–69) 202–204.

71   "Make Marcus Marius": *CIL* 4.3. "The goldsmiths": *CIL* 4.710 (cf. Lewis-Reinhold 237). "Satia and Petronia": *CIL* 4.3294 (cf. Lewis-Reinhold 237). "Genialis urges": *CIL* 4.3702 (cf. Lewis-Reinhold 238). *"Dormientes"*: *CIL* 4.575. *"Seri Bibi"*: *CIL* 4.581. "Sneak-Thieves": *CIL* 4.576. *"Verus Innocens"*: *CIL* 4.1080.

72   "The troop of gladiators": *CIL* 4.1189. "In the Arrius Pollio block": *CIL* 4.138 (cf. Homo 519). "A copper pot": *CIL* 4.64 (cf. Lewis-Reinhold 277). Winning bets, number of steps: Mau-Kelsey 487. *"Paris hic"*: *CIL* 4.1305. *"Staphilus hic"*: *CIL* 4.4087, 2060. Obscenities: *CIL* 4.1255, 1425, 1441, 1503. ABC's: *CIL* 4.2514–2548. "Lovers, like bees": *CIL* 4.8408. "I marvel": *CIL* 4.1904 (cf. Mau-Kelsey 481).

73–75   Ostia's history: Meiggs 20–34. Population: Meiggs 533–535. Ruins chiefly second A.D.: Meiggs 14. Apartment houses: Meiggs 67–69. Garden apartments: Meiggs 139, 245 (plan). Public baths short distance away: The Terme Marittime; see C. Pavolini, *Ostia³* (Bari 1983) 162. Baths at Ostia: Meiggs 418. Nature of population: Meiggs 196–211. Piazzale delle Corporazioni: Meiggs 283–287; Casson 153. Builders' Association: Meiggs 324.

75–76   Growth of the port area: Meiggs 86–89. Urban blight: Meiggs 85, 252. Brief revival: Meiggs 92–95. End of Ostia: Meiggs 97–101.

Chapter VIII. The Soldier

77   "Dear Father": *Sel. Pap.*, no. 112.

78–79   Hitch: Watson 102. Augustus founds standing army: Watson 11. Size of army, of legions: Watson 13, 15. Colonials: Watson 15. Gain citizenship: Watson 136, 154. Praetorians: Watson 16–18. Navy: Starr 66–74.

79 Location of legions: Watson 14–15. Men spend life near base: Watson 148.

79–81 Recruits: Watson 37–41. Travel money: Watson 44. Training: Watson 54–72. Little combat: Watson 143–145. "I thank Serapis": H. Youtie and J. Winter, *Michigan Papyri* viii (Ann Arbor 1951), no. 465.13–17. Another letter: Youtie-Winter viii, no. 466.22–30.

81–82 Promotion: Watson 75–77. Noncommissioned ranks: Watson 78–79. *cornicularius*: Watson 85–86. Centurions: Watson 86–88. Commanding officers: Watson 23–24.

82 Legionaries' pay: Watson 90–92. Augustus's will: Watson 98. Tiberius's will: Watson 109. Separation pay: Watson 147–149. Auxiliaries' and sailors' pay: Watson 99–102. Praetorians' pay: Watson 97–99. Donatives: Watson 109–111. Auction of the emperorship: Watson 111–112. Severus's reform: Watson 17.

83 Prohibition of marriage, quasi-legitimacy of children: Watson 133–136. Settle down where based: Watson 144, 153. Replaced by sons: Dill 208; Starr 95. Profit by help from fathers: Watson 37. Veterans' status in local society: Dill 215–216. "been honorably discharged": *ILS* 6957 (cf. Lewis-Reinhold 260).

Chapter IX. Many Gods

84 Secularization of Roman religion: cf. Dill 529–530, 533, 545. "Oh, dear": Suetonius, *Vespasian* 23.4.

85 Cult of Hercules: Dill 538. Syncretism, Belatucader: D. Dudley, *The Civilization of Rome* (NAL 1960) 229. Jupiter Dolichenus: Watson 132.

85–88 From city-state deities to eastern deities: Tarn-Griffith 337. Isis: Dill 560–584. Her appeal to women: Tarn-Griffith 359. "I am Isis": *Syll.*³ 1267. Syncretism of Isis with Greek goddesses: Tarn-Griffith 357; Dill 581. Her titles: Tarn-Griffith 357–358. Path to Rome and difficulties there: Dill 563, 565. Shrine of Isis, obelisks: E. Nash, *Pictorial Dictionary of Ancient Rome*² (New York 1968) i 510, ii 148–152, 159. Nile water: Juvenal 6.526–529. Services: Dill 577–578. Cult image, festivals: Tarn-Griffith 358; Lewis-Reinhold 543–545. Clergy: Dill 582–583. The "call": Tarn-Griffith 358.

88–89 Serapis: Tarn-Griffith 356–357. Cybele: Dill 547–559. Syncretism with Astarte: Dill 558. Legend of love for Atthis: Dill 549–550. Proces-

sion: Grant 192–194. Excesses toned down: Meiggs 356, 360–362. New
respectable priesthood: Dill 550–551. Augustine saw them: *de Civitate
Dei* 7.26. *taurobolium*: Meiggs 362–363; Grant 195. *"in aeternum renatus"*:
ILS 4152.

89–90   Eleusinian, Dionysiac Mysteries: Grant 186–189. Villa of the Mysteries: op cit. 58–60.

90–92   Mithraism: Dill 585–626. Nature and rule of Mithras: Dill 586–587.
Struggle with the bull: Grant 201. Grades of initiates: Dill 611. Chapels:
Dill 613–614. Costumes and sounds: Grant 203. Congregations small:
Dill 613; Meiggs 372. Mithraea in Rome: Grant 203; Nash (op. cit.
under 85–88) ii 69–85. In Ostia: Meiggs 370. Moral demands: Dill 608–
609. Appeal to army men: Grant 204; Watson 132–133. Christianity's
rival: Dill 622; Meiggs 389.

92–94   Astrology: Tarn-Griffith 345–352. Augustus's and Domitian's coins,
Tiberius's companion, Commodus's bust: Grant 167–169. Banning of
astrologers: Grant 167. Lucian's dialogue: Lucian, *Dial. Mort.* 30 (cf.
Grant 155). Carneades: Tarn-Griffith 348. Outwit the stars: Grant 165–
166. Horoscopes found in Egypt: *Sel. Pap.* 199, 200. "I alone may prolong": Apuleius, *Met.* 11.6.

94–97   Magic: Tarn-Griffith 352–353; Grant 173–176. "I call thee,
Hermes": *Greek Papyri in the British Museum* i (London 1893), no.
46.173–195 (cf. Lewis-Reinhold 533). "the remains of human bodies":
Tacitus, *Ann.* 2.69.5. Dream interpretations: Dill 467–471. Oracles:
Dill, 434, 471–477. "Am I to remain": *Sel. Pap.*, no. 195. "The fame of
the shrine": Lucian, *Alexander* 30–31. Pliny comforts Suetonius: Lucian,
1.18. Ides of March: Suetonius, *Caesar* 81.2. Portents: Suetonius, *Augustus* 97.1–2, *Tiberius* 74, *Caligula* 57.

Chapter X. Fun and Games

98–99   "Serve him wine": Vergil, *Copa* 37. Knucklebones, pictures of dice
games, Augustus's skill: Balsdon 154–155. Claudius's carriage: Suetonius,
Claudius 33.2. "The die is cast": Suetonius, *Caesar* 32. Expensive gaming
tables, game boards scratched, philosopher in jail: Balsdon 158–159.

99–100   Sports: Balsdon 160–168. Handball: Balsdon 165–166. *ludi*: Balsdon 245–248. Theatre seats: Balsdon 258–260. Contracts: Balsdon
281–283 (actors), 315 (charioteers).

100–101   Mime: Balsdon 276–278. *modo egens*: Cicero, *Phil.* 2.65. Equivalent of Jesse James: Suetonius, *Caligula* 57.4. Vaudeville acts: Balsdon

287–288. "Bring on a bear": Horace, *Epist.* 2.1.185–186. Pantomime: Balsdon 274–276. Chaos to Cleopatra: Lucian, *Salt.* 37. Police force, Nero's removal: Balsdon 266. Actors' status: Balsdon 282–283.

101–103   "bread and circuses": Juvenal 10.81. Capacity of Circus Maximus: Balsdon 268. Pliny's attitude: Balsdon 9.6. Emperors as racing fans: H. Harris, *Sport in Greece and Rome* (Ithaca 1972) 214–217. Trimalchio's cook: Petronius 70.13. Length of races, teams: Balsdon 316–317. Stables: Balsdon 314–315. Greens the favorite: Balsdon 321. Gloom when Greens lose: Juvenal 11.197–201. The horses: Balsdon 315. Fixing races: Balsdon 318. "I conjure you": *IGRR* i, no. 117 (cf. Lewis–Reinhold 534). Caligula: Dio Cassius 59.14.5–6. Racetrack seating: Balsdon 321. Picking up a girl: Ovid, *Ars Am.* 1.135–163. Courier-swallows: Pliny, *HN* 10.71. 1462 firsts: *ILS* 5287 (cf. Balsdon 322–323, Harris 198–201).

103–104   Gladiatorial contests: Balsdon 248–251. Titus's contests: Dio Cassius 66.25.1. Trajan's contests: Dio Cassius 68.15.1. Colosseum's arrangements: Balsdon 259–261; Lanciani (op. cit. under 38–40) 379–383. Seating, barring of women: Suetonius, *Augustus* 44.2. Awnings: Balsdon 257–258. Handled by sailors: Starr 20–21. Safety precautions: Balsdon 311.

104–108   Brought from Etruria to Rome: Balsdon 248–249. Profitable investment: Balsdon 292. Schools, recruitment, women gladiators: Balsdon 288–293. Training, types of fighters: Balsdon 294–295. Marriages, love affairs: Balsdon 296–297. *suspirium puellarum*: *CIL* 4.4342. Testing if dead: Balsdon 301. Duels to the death: Livy 41.20.12; Suetonius, *Augustus* 45.3. Appeal for mercy: Balsdon 3000. Number of fights: Balsdon 301–302. "to the sword," slaughtering: Balsdon 288–289, 308. Killing of animals: Balsdon 309–313. Numbers killed: Balsdon 307–308.

108   Amphitheatres used for bullfights: For example, at Nîmes and Arles in southern France. Intellectuals' attitudes: Balsdon 298–299. Constantine's decree: Balsdon 251.

Chapter XI. On the Road

109–110   "I am well": *Sel. Pap.*, no. 113. Objects of trade: Casson, *AM* 198–199. 135,000 tons: Casson, *AM* 207. Use of government roads: Casson 164. Africa, India trade: Casson, *AM* 202–206. "honest in their transactions," "the ninth year": F. Hirth, *China and the Roman Orient* (Shanghai 1885, repr. Chicago 1967) 42.

110–114   Traveling for health: Casson 130–134. "Many throughout Sicily": Diodorus 5.10.1. Festival travel: Casson 136–137. Vacationers: Casson 138–148. Cicero's villas: Casson 138–139. His neighbors: Casson 139–141. Baiae: Casson 142–143. "filled the lakes": Seneca, *Ep.* 51.4. "Unmarried girls": Varro ap. Nonius 154.4. "Why must I look": Seneca, *Ep.* 51.4. "to the squabbles": Seneca, *Ep.* 51.12. "The wife, even worse": Martial 1.62. Augustus's attitude toward Baiae: Casson 143. Hill retreats: Casson 145–146. Horace's, Martial's villa: Casson 146–147. "So, Pannychus": Martial 12.72. "Is he homeward bound": Martial 3.47.15.

114–116   Travel by sea: Casson 149–162. Travel by land: Casson 176–182. Commodus's swiveling seat: Casson 181.

116–118   Inns: Casson 197–211. "Lucius Memmius": *Sel. Pap.*, no. 416.3–11. *cursus publicus*: Casson 182–190. Tabula Peutingeriana: Casson 186–188. "Innkeeper, I pissed": *CIL* 4.4957. Meals: Casson 211–218. Galen's statement: *de Simp. Medic.* 10.2.2 (Kuhn xii, 254). "The rains this year": Martial 1.56.

118–122   Tourists: Casson chapters 14–19. "Since many these days": Casson 360. Sights to see: Casson 229–237. Temple-museums: Casson 238–252. Homer country: Casson 256. Egypt: Casson 257–261. Guidebooks: Casson 292–299. Guides: Casson 264–267. "The guides went through": Plutarch, *Mor.* 395a. "Zeus, protect me": Varro, ap. Nonius 419.4. "Abolish fabulous tales": Lucian, *Philops.* 4. Local performances: Casson 271. Memnon: Casson 272–278. "He has learned": A. and E. Bernand, *Les inscriptions grecques et latines du colosse de Memnon* (Cairo 1960), no. 61. "I heard the wonderful": Bernand no. 34.

123–124   Shopping: Casson 286–291. "If my health": *Sel. Pap.*, no. 170.22–27. Customs: Casson 290–291. "Send . . . a bathing": *Sel. Pap.*, no. 88.7–11.

Chapter XII. The Engineer

125   "The Romans have made": Strabo 5.235. Etruscan accomplishments: J. Ward-Perkins in *Hommages à Albert Grenier* (Brussels 1962) 1636–1643.

126   Rome's highways: Casson 163–175. "were carried straight": Plutarch, *Gaius Gracchus* 7.1.

126–128   Early history of the arch: L. Crema, *L'architettura romana (Enciclopedia Classica,* Sezione iii, Volume xii, Tomo I, Turin 1959) 9–10. Theatre holding 20,000: R. Stillwell, ed., *The Princeton Encyclopedia of Classical Sites* (Princeton 1976) 575 (Megalopolis). Augustus's program:

Ward-Perkins 183–201. Romans' first uses of the arch: Ward-Perkins 102, 174–175. The commemorative arch: Crema 100–104. First uses of concrete, Tiber warehouse: Ward-Perkins 106–107. Vaults in theatres: Ward-Perkins 170–173, 188. Domes: Ward-Perkins 163.

128–129   Roman concrete, techniques for building concrete walls: Ward-Perkins 246–247. Exterior finishes: Ward-Perkins 117, 143, 262 (stucco), 260 (marble). Columns and pediments as decoration: Ward-Perkins 188, 261.

130   Expedition to the Nile: M. Cary and E. Warmington, *The Ancient Explorers*[2] (Penguin 1963) 211–212. Stomach medicine: Marcellus, *de Medicamentis* 20.84. Lens: Pliny, *HN* 37.64. Water organ: Suetonius, *Nero* 41.2. Baths: Ward-Perkins 211–212. Canal: Suetonius, *Nero* 19.2. Waterway: Suetonius, *Nero* 31.3; Tacitus, *Ann.* 15.42.2. Rebuilding of Rome: Tacitus, *Ann.* 15.43. Golden House: Ward-Perkins 248–251.

130–132   Hadrian's villa: Ward-Perkins 254–256. "Go draw your pumpkins": Dio Cassius 69.4.2. Pantheon: Ward-Perkins 256–260. Imperial baths: Ward-Perkins 271–273, 500–502. Michelangelo's church: Santa Maria degli Angeli.

132–133   Basilicas and Christian churches: Ward-Perkins 243–244. St. John Lateran: R. Krautheimer, *Rome: Profile of a City, 312–1308* (Princeton 1980) 22. Concrete aqueducts: Ward-Perkins 209. Colosseum's structure: Ward-Perkins 223. Harbor north of Ostia: L. Casson, *Ships and Seamanship in the Ancient World*[3] (Baltimore 1995) 367–369.

134   "A man of letters": Vitruvius 1.1.3. "it teaches us": Vitruvius 1.1.4. "he should be able": Vitruvius 1.1.5. "it makes an architect": Vitruvius 1.1.7. Tune catapults: Vitruvius 1.1.8. "of air, the healthiness," regulations, sundials: Vitruvius 1.1.10.

134–135   Avoid marshes for city sites: Vitruvius 1.4.1. "if they are cold": Vitruvius 1.6.1. Siting of theatres: Vitruvius 5.3.1–2. Siting of baths: Vitruvius 5.10.1. Climate and houses: Vitruvius 6.1.2. Proportions of public buildings: Cf. Vitruvius 4.4 (temples). Stuccoing, painting: Vitruvius 7.3–5. Dimensions of columns: Cf. Vitruvius 5.1.6 (basilicas). Dimensions of pipes: Vitruvius 8.6.4. Design of derricks: Vitruvius 10.2–3. Design of waterclocks: Vitruvius 9.8.

Chapter XIII. The Emperor

137   Renounced campaign in the east: Henderson 138–140. "He desired peace": S.H.A., *Hadrian* 10.2. Army reforms: Henderson 171–177.

Speech at Lambaesis: Henderson 94–98. Lives like a soldier: S.H.A., *Hadrian* 10.2–5. Strengthening of frontiers: Henderson 141–147. Wall in Britain: Henderson 151–167.

138–139   Hadrian's return: Henderson 43. Travels: Henderson 294. Farm legislation: Henderson 98–101. Alcibiades's tomb: Athenaeus 13.574f. Temple at Nîmes, at Tarragona: Henderson 83. Hadrianopolises: Henderson 85. Rebuilding of towns: Henderson 85–86. Temple at Cyzicus: Henderson 86. Report on the Black Sea: Arrian, *Periplus ponti Euxini*. Baths and aqueduct at Corinth: Henderson 108. Eleusis: Henderson 112–113. Athens: Henderson 113–119.

139   Jewish War: Henderson 213–230. Bar-Kokhba revolt's survivors: Y. Yadin, *Bar-Kokhba* (London 1971) 62–65.

139–140   Codification: A. Berger, *Encyclopedic Dictionary of Roman Law* (Philadelphia 1953) s.v. "Edictum perpetuum Hadriani." Reform of government bureaucracy: Henderson 64–67. Suetonius's clerkship: Henderson 67 n. 2. Suetonius fired: Henderson 23. Hadrian's beard: Henderson 24.

140–141   Temple of Venus and Rome: Ward-Perkins 265–266. Temple to his mother-in-law: Nash (op. cit. under 85–88) s.v. "Matidia, Templum." Pontifex Maximus: S.H.A., *Hadrian* 22.10. Restoration of sanctuaries: Henderson 107. Festival to Dionysus: Dio Cassius 69.16.1–2. Consulted Delphic Oracle: Henderson 111. Believer in astrology: Dill 503. Foresaw his own death: S.H.A., *Hadrian* 16.7.

141–143   Antinous: Henderson 130–134. Relations with his wife: Henderson 22–25. Multiple statues of Antinous: Cf. S. Perowne, *Hadrian* (London 1960) 99.

143–144   "He was an ardent": S.H.A., *Hadrian* 14.8–11. Passion for hunting: Henderson 16–18. Slaughter of beasts: Henderson 113. Selling of Jewish captives: Henderson 218. Sculptor and artist: Henderson 237. Villa at Tivoli: op cit. under 130–132. Tomb: Ward-Perkins 266–267.

144–146   Hadrian and literature: Henderson 240–246. Autobiography: Henderson 242. "Caesar would I": S.H.A., *Hadrian* 16.3–4. His death: Henderson 264–265. Naming of Pius: Henderson 261. *"Animula"*: S.H.A., *Hadrian* 25.9. "Stick together": Dio Cassius 77.15.2.

Index